France and the French

FRANCE AND
THE FRENCH

Harvey Edwards

THOMAS NELSON INC.
Nashville / New York

Acknowledgments

The author would like to thank the French Government Tourist Office and the French Embassy in New York for granting him permission to use their photographs. Other photos were taken by the author and by photographer Del Mulkey.

All rights reserved under International and Pan-American Conventions. Published in Nashville, Tennessee, by Thomas Nelson Inc. and simultaneously in Don Mills, Ontario, by Thomas Nelson & Sons (Canada) Limited.

Library of Congress Catalog Card Number: 73-169038
International Standard Book Number: 0-8407-7064-2
                    0-8407-7065-0 NLB

Printed in the United States of America

Acknowledgments

In the realization of this book, the following persons have been extremely helpful: M. René Bardy and Mr. Myron Clement at the French National Tourist Office, New York; M. Edouard Morot-Sir, French Embassy, New York; M. Jean Carbonnet, French Cultural Service, New York; M. Jacquemain, Chef du Bureau d'Accueil, Commissariat Général au Tourisme, Paris; M. Louis Gillette, Chef du Bureau de l'Accueil, of the Ministère des Affaires Étrangères, Paris; M. Leherpeux, l'Institut Pédagogique National, Paris; M. Doise, Service de Presse du Ministère des Affaires Étrangères, Paris.

Special thanks must go to Mme. Denise Bévière and the Conseil National du Patronat Français, who arranged many visits to factories and research centers throughout France; M. Maroselli, Press Chief of the Régie Nationale des Usines Renault at Boulogne-Billancourt; M. Roche of the French National Railroads, Paris; and to my good friends M. and Mme. Pierre Boulat of Paris for their frequent warm welcomes and good advice.

ENGLAND

HOLLAND

BELGIUM

CALAIS

LILLE

The Channel

CHERBOURG

LE HAVRE

ROUEN

LUXEMBOURG

GERMANY

RHINE

SEINE

MARNE

PARIS

STRASBOURG

BREST

ORLÉANS

SEINE

RHINE

NANTES

LOIRE

FRANCE

SWITZERLAND

SAÔNE

Atlantic

LA ROCHELLE

GENEVA

RHÔNE

Ocean

LOIRE

LYONS

ITALY

ALLIER

ISÈRE

BORDEAUX

DORDOGNE

RHÔNE

LOT

DURANCE

GARONNE

AVIGNON

TOULOUSE

MARSEILLES

NICE

ARIÈGE

NARBONNE

TOULON

BASTIA

SPAIN

Mediterranean Sea

CORSICA

AJACCIO

MAP OF FRANCE

Legend:

● Cities

- - - - - National Frontiers

〜〜〜 Rivers

N

Contents

A Notre Dame Cathedral gargoyle leers out over the Paris scene: automobiles, the Seine River, and, far in the background, the Eiffel Tower.

Introduction

I first came to France in 1949. Because I liked it then, I came back in 1958. For the past five years, with my French wife and our two children, I have lived in Chamonix, in the beautiful French Alps. I like to think of the town, which is a world-renowned mountaineering center and ski resort, as a microcosm of French life, that the daily life of Chamonix more or less reflects what occurs in small towns all over the country and, on a reduced scale, what takes place in the big cities as well.

In some ways, this is true. Chamonix has a *boulangerie,* where we buy the long French bread that is a staple of every French table; a *boucherie,* where we buy our meat; and several *épiceries,* or grocery stores. There's a post office in the center of town, the city hall, a tourist office, and, not far off, a war memorial. On Saturday mornings in Chamonix, as in thousands of other French towns and in the big cities as well, there is an outdoor market in the town square, where we meet our friends and can buy almost anything—clothing, toys, vegetables, flowers, fish, or cheeses from all over the country. There is an animation to a French market that is human and exciting; for me, the market is the great continuing stream of French life. All social classes mix there, and in a way, life itself is replenished. Townspeople talk of the weather, the prices, the latest marriages, births, or scandals, of a new car bought, or even of political events, while the cries of the merchants are heard above all. But through all the confusion, there is a certain order and rhythm which is given to the day. Another reason why I like the

Narrow old streets where shoppers stop to exchange news and gossip can be seen in towns all over France.

markets of France is because they are so traditional: markets very similar to these have existed for hundreds of years.

At noontime, the firehouse siren is tested and the women are back home feeding the children, while the *pommes frites* are browning in the hot peanut oil. In the evenings, on Sundays and holidays, or whenever there is a marriage or funeral, the church bells echo from one side of the valley to the other. France is a Catholic country, but Catholicism, like communism, exists in different versions in different parts of the world. During the week the children go to school; the men—and more and more women—hurry to and from work. There's quick pause in a café for a *petit rouge* or an *apéritif* before the big noon meal. The smells of French cooking fill the streets and lanes; the women swing their metal baskets to shake the last drops of water from the salad leaves. After dinner, the newspaper is read for the national news and, even more important in a small town, for the local news. In the evenings, after the soup and omelette, the cheese, wine, and fruit, there is radio and television. But the French people tend to go to bed early, particularly in the country.

Weekends are for family visits. The grandparents come, who inevitably spoil the children, and there are discussions, jokes, and polite criticism around the table. In a country town, people have more time for traditional family life; but even in Paris, Lyons, Marseilles, and other large French cities, the feeling for family ties is strong.

In many ways, however, the quiet provincial life—so important during the eighteenth and nineteenth centuries—is no longer representative of the life of France. Today the cities, particularly Paris, dominate the French scene. Through radio, TV, the newspapers and magazines, French men and women in the small towns from Normandy in the north to the Côte d'Azur on the Mediterranean Sea in the south, from the tip of Brittany in the west to Strasbourg in the industrial east are quickly made aware of the fact that much is going on around them, even outside their borders, which may eventually affect their lives. Provincialism, so closely related to isolationism, has become almost an attitude of the past.

The French know that there are serious problems in agriculture,

Medieval Strasbourg, clustered about the cathedral and embraced by the Ill River, presents an urban landscape of unusual charm.

education, and industry. For many years, prices have been rising; inflation and unemployment are constant dangers. All the effects of the 1968 general strike, euphemistically called a revolution, have not yet become clear. Many promises were made by a government under duress, a government which, with the departure of General de Gaulle, is made up of men who claim to have different ideas and new ways of doing things. Will the new government, with Georges Pompidou as president, be strong enough to institute meaningful reforms that will calm the turbulent French spirit; or will France, after ten years of semidictatorial rule by de Gaulle, once again slip into an era of in-fighting by political parties and private interest groups? One thing is clear: Social unrest has once again become a part of the French scene.

Important issues—and less important ones—are considered in small towns and cities all over France. But unlike many other countries in

which there are several important cities, in France the major political, economic, and social decisions are made in Paris, the capital. What is decided there affects all Frenchmen. Paris is where the legislature meets, where the central government offices are; it houses the stock and grain markets, the home offices of banks, of public and private industry, of labor unions; it has the largest newspapers, most of the country's radio and television studios, and important universities. Paris, the most populated and most beautiful city in France, is the intellectual and cultural capital of the country, perhaps of Europe.

France is in a state of rapid change. The people are trying to catch up with their European neighbors and to compete with the American giant. Old institutions are giving way to new ones, and new ways of thinking are developing. While this is going on, the French are seeking a new identity, and the country is struggling to find its true role in a turbulent world.

To understand what it means when an American-style supermarket takes the place of *boulangeries, épiceries,* and *boucheries,* we must investigate the roots of French life. We must consider ideas and attitudes that go back centuries, some as old as the establishment of France itself. The character of the people who formed and settled the country two thousand years ago is reflected in the French language of today. France's complex history—the wars, the revolutions, the thousand years of monarchy, the hundred years of republican government—affect the people's attitudes toward one another. The country's geographical position has in large part determined France's attitude toward its neighbors as well as its once huge colonial empire. Even the weather has its effect not only on the crops but on the mood of the farmer as well.

In preparing this book, photographer Del Mulkey and I traveled from the small town of Chamonix to many of the cities and regions of France. I talked with and recorded the conversations of farmers, fishermen, industrial workers, scientists, government employees, artists, sportsmen, educators, teachers, labor leaders, and students.

To the French men and women who contributed so much, to my wife and her family, who taught me more about French life than many scholarly volumes, this book is dedicated.

Old and new can be seen side by side in Paris. Here, a man with a wheelbarrow crosses the street in front of the modern Radio and Television building.

The French Personality

France contains two fundamental temperaments—that of the left and that of the right; three principal tendencies, if one adds the center; six spiritual families; ten parties, large or small, traversed by multiple currents; fourteen parliamentary groups without much discipline; and forty million opinions.—JACQUES FAUVET

When I first came to France more than twenty years ago, I was struck by the country's age. Notre Dame and Chartres cathedrals were almost five hundred years older than anything I had ever seen before, and the Luxembourg Gardens, where children sailed boats or played in the symmetrical squares and tree-lined walks, represented a formalism I had never known.

The monuments and parks still remain to be admired, but since World War Two the overall appearance of the land of the Gauls has changed more rapidly than ever before. Airplanes, automobiles, skyscrapers, and all they bring with them—airports, noise, roads, gasoline stations, crowded cities—have changed the physical aspect of the country and, in some respects, the way of life. Still, the thinking of the French, colored as it is by more than a thousand years of nationhood, has not changed as easily as the country's physical characteristics. This is not to say that the French live exclusively in the past. Their life is a strange mixture of the past and present; and when the chips are down, when war, revolution, or extremism of any kind threatens traditional French life, the people have a tendency to turn nationalistic

The lined face of farmer Charles François expresses years of hard work, but a touch of humor and the indomitable French spirit shine forth from his eyes.

17

and conservative. Then they evoke their ancient traditions, recall their history, and often prefer the old to the new.

The Sense of the Past

In France, the past is omnipresent. Small towns and cities more often than not are laid out around a central *place,* or square, near which one finds a stone church or cathedral built in medieval or Renaissance times. Southern French cities like Arles, Marseilles, Nîmes, and Orange, with their stone walls and towers, their ancient baths, amphitheaters, moats, and bridges reflect the influence of the Roman conquest, which took place between 123 and 54 B.C. In Marseilles, France's second-largest city, founded by the Greeks around 600 B.C., remains of ancient civilizations are still being unearthed. Just recently the city of Paris decided to build an underground parking lot in front of Notre Dame Cathedral. Work was halted when ancient walls from Roman times were discovered. Despite the urgent need for more automobile parking space, archaeologists began a "dig."

Hundreds of examples of the ancient existing with, or struggling against, the modern can be found in France. In the old part of Lyons, where the cobblestone streets are almost as narrow as the wagons were wide in olden times, I visited a sixteenth-century home owned by a young couple. They had completely restored the interior: high ceilings and decorated beams. But on a Louis XIV table was a modern telephone, and a refrigerator-freezer was partially hidden behind a curtain. They were proud of their home; at the same time, they complained about how difficult it was to heat and keep clean.

The French, like most European peoples, have a deep sense of the past. Instinctively and through training, they know that their country is old and has had a long, often perilous, history. A Frenchman sitting down to his Sunday dinner of *poule au pot* (chicken in the pot), may well remark that it was King Henry IV who said, back in the sixteenth century, "Every Frenchman should have a fowl in the pot on Sunday." French schoolchildren learn history with the thoroughness of monks, even to such things as memorizing the dates of the reigns of the kings of France, the names of the ninety-five *départements,* or counties, the

A father parades his small child in the arena at Arles, where bullfights are still held.

many wars fought, and the tactical maneuvers of both sides in the Battle of Austerlitz.

In other ways, as well, the past infiltrates into the current life of the people. It is hammered home through celebrations of armistice days and the debarkment of allied troops. In magazine and newspaper articles and radio and TV programs the past grandeur of France is a frequent theme, and nostalgia is aroused for the glorious times when France led the world in political power and military might, in fashion and style, and in science and philosophy and the fine arts.

Out of this ever-present sense of the past, two important strains of the French personality have grown: a deep-seated nationalism and a tendency to be conservative. In a country that is changing more rapidly than ever before, both of these characteristics are under attack.

Patriotism is alive in almost every French heart, but modern develop-

About 136 people live in the picturesque village of Mount Saint-Michel which is connected to the coast by a long dike. Dating from the twelfth century, it consists of a church, a cloister, and a refectory.

ments have, so to speak, turned the French against themselves. With the growth of the European Common Market, France has become more integrated into Europe, in the economic sense at least. Businessmen, farmers, labor-union leaders, even factory workers realize that the French economy is tied up with the economics of five other European powers. French bankers and financiers are faced with worldwide money markets. They are forced to take into account developments in the United States and other parts of the world as well. For the first time, industrialists are beginning to compete on a large scale not only for European but for world markets. Research workers, engineers, and students are more aware of important discoveries in other parts of the world. Now the Frenchman on vacation has a tendency not only to visit the châteaux of the Loire or picturesque Mont Saint-Michel but to go beyond the borders of France to foreign lands. Thus, the very frontiers

20

of France have been enlarged, and with them the scope of French thinking.

European economic cooperation has become a fact in modern French life. But can this cooperation be extended to the political sphere? Will there someday be a European union of states similar to our United States, with one unifying legislature which, in principle, treats general rather than individual interests? If this ever comes to be, France and the French will have to go through some radical changes. The nationalism, still so rampant all over the country, will have to be toned down. In any case, the increased contact with other peoples and their ideas that has taken place since the end of World War Two is a step forward. It is helping the French to reconsider their world image.

Suspicion of One-Man Rule

Two fundamental ideas of government grew out of the French Revolution of 1789. First, the personal power of the king and his regents was undermined and, for all practical purposes, destroyed. In the years to come there would be reemergences of monarchy, but never again would a French king have such power. That power was eventually entrusted to the National Assembly. Secondly, the Revolution weakened the role of the church, because it had been the church that supported monarchy and proclaimed that the king was appointed by God. The governing power that was unleashed was eventually absorbed by the state.

Unfortunately, despots like Napoleon III, Bonaparte's nephew, Cavaignac, MacMahon, and Boulanger, who worked more or less within the new system of government, used their power against the interests of the people. As a result, the many centuries of tyranny in France continued and has led to the modern Frenchman's suspicion of government and any authority.

Inherently, the people today prefer a weak government to a strong one, which often meant tyranny in the past. And this explains why skepticism, even cynicism, about what the government can accomplish is very much a part of French character. In addition, 175 years of unstable and uncertain governments have had a great deal to do with the slowness of the growth of industries and has kept France, potentially one of the richest countries of Europe, behind her European neighbors in many important respects.

The French Civilizing Mission

By nature, the French are conservative people. They are attached to their country, the region in which they live, and their homes. They like good cooking, which has tremendous importance in French life. They like life to have continuity, repetition, order. And they are infinitely proud of the fact that they are French. When they travel abroad they like to compare whatever they see to things French. More often than not, they prefer the life back home. They are proud of their past, cynical about the present, and uncommitted regarding the future. Whatever is new or progressive comes under attack, not because it is necessarily bad, but because it does not conform with the past.

Part of the reason for this comes from their belief that their civilization, their way of life is superior to all others. In many ways and at certain moments in history it has been. For 150 years, during the seventeenth and eighteenth centuries, France was the dominant European power. French ideas and customs spread throughout Europe. The French language was spoken at all the courts, and it was fashionable for other languages to be sprinkled with French expressions. French was the language of the diplomats and the peace treaties.

When the colonies were established, the idea of French prestige was held to be more important than settlement or economic exploitation. Spreading the French way of life—language, culture, art, music, and so forth—gave the people prestige and supported the national image. When French people went abroad, they did so not to be integrated into the foreign country; they went to spread the French way of life, which was "the right way." The colonists believed that France had a civilizing mission. This holier-than-thou attitude and nostalgia for the great past, together with nationalism and traditionalism, is latent in the French character.

One of the things the government boasted about in the 1960's was the rapidity with which half a million French Algerians were integrated into the French stream of life. What the government meant by integration was that so many French Algerians did not and could not influence or change the French way of life. The French still have a tendency to absorb or incorporate other cultures and peoples and to resist changing themselves.

Conflicts and Paradoxes

The French are vibrant, passionate, individualistic, often ingenious people. In order to survive in a country full of red tape and a growing bureaucratization, they have developed a certain quality they call *débrouillard*—a practically untranslatable word. In effect, it means that despite the terrible odds against them, French people are able to get things done. Many obstacles attend the simple act of applying for a government-built apartment, getting a telephone (the French telephone company is probably the only company in France which consistently discourages clients), obtaining a building permit from the *préfecture* (the

A young Portuguese apprentice, Fernando Augusta, is learning to lay cobblestones. Much of France's manual work is now done by Portuguese, Spaniards, and Algerians, who are tempted into France because of higher salaries than they could get at home.

23

county seat of government), getting a low-interest loan, or, for the several million foreign workers in the country, obtaining the work permit without which they cannot legally lift a stone for pay. These daily matters involving the individual's dealings with the government are complicated and full of problems. They are resolved by using the influence of relatives and friends (*pistonnage* is the French expression), no matter how distant; an occasional well-placed *pourboire,* or gratuity; or simply being so persistent that a tiny part of the structure gives way and doors finally open.

His language has provided the Frenchman with a potent weapon. The skills of persuasion, the art of reasoning, even creative argot are pushed to their limits until that moment of supreme triumph: The applicant emerges from the bureau with the desired paper. The more adept one is at obtaining the impossible, the more *débrouillard* one is. In the eyes of the French, this quality is more desirable than winning a million francs in the national lottery.

Complementing the *débrouillard* quality, which concerns getting things done or obtaining special favors, is a second French quality which may or may not be traceable to the French Revolution and the emergence of the Frenchman as an individual. This is the quality of being *malin,* another hard-to-define word. The dictionary says that *malin* can mean evil-minded, wicked, malicious, shrewd, or cunning. But these English synonyms do not really convey the larger everyday sense of the word.

The American humorist Art Buchwald, who spent the first fourteen years of his journalistic career covering the French scene, gave this example of what it meant to be *malin.* After having tried in various circles to obtain a satisfactory definition, in despair he asked a nine-year-old boy. After reflection, the boy said, "If some of us are playing tug-of-war in the Tuileries Gardens, and I tie our end of the rope to a tree, that is *malin.*"

The *débrouillard* and *malin* qualities have probably been more effective in getting the individual Frenchman through hard times than anything else. In a country where "having connections" has often been more important than justice and talent, they are indispensable devices for survival.

Boys playing on a steep flight of stairs in Montmartre, which is famous for its artist colony.

The French personality is full of conflicts. The French esteem the past; at the same time, they recognize the advantages, even the necessity, for change. On the one hand, they are suspicious of government or any authority; on the other, they know that they need the government, which protects them against many of the abuses of the past. While the individual is the most important factor in French society, group action has become more and more common. These conflicts and paradoxes make the people fascinating human beings. Wherever a Frenchman is present, you can be sure there is animation. You may not agree with what he has to say, but he will express himself with wit, humor, and passion. And for the French, these three qualities are essential.

25

The Formation of France

The French imagine the universe as a huge vague circle in the center of which is Paris.—HENRI BIDOU

The shape of France has often been described as hexagonal. Except for the northeast border with Belgium and Luxembourg, the boundaries of France are natural ones. The English Channel, which the French call *La Manche,* separates France from Great Britain, the Pyrenees separate it from Spain, the Alps from Italy, the Jura Mountains from Switzerland, and the Rhine River from Germany. The west coast borders the Atlantic Ocean and extends to Spain; in the south, the Mediterranean coastline goes all the way to Italy. In all, there are more than eighteen hundred miles of French coastline, with well-protected ports capable of handling supertankers as well as fishing fleets and small pleasure boats.

In area about 212,000 square miles without the Mediterranean island of Corsica, France is smaller than the state of Texas, but its physical features are much more varied. There are rolling farmlands and flat plains, mountains where the snow is eternal, hills formed by volcanos, deep valleys, and dark forests. The principal rivers—the Seine, the Loire, the Rhone, the Saône, and the Garonne—are navigable. Through a system of inland canals it is possible to pilot a small boat from Dunkirk in the north to Marseilles in the south. Even more important for the country's economic life is that on many of the rivers and their tributaries, thousands of tons of building materials, hydrocarbons, coal,

The narrow cobblestoned streets in Vence, near Nice, are right out of the Middle Ages.

The tight and dry Brittany houses are made of local stone with steep pitched roofs. With rain falling on an average of about two hundred days in a year, the region is one of the wettest in France.

and agricultural products are regularly transported by some nine thousand lighters.

Weather

France has a temperate climate, but there are some extremes from time to time that make the climate rather varied. The country lies in the middle of the northern temperate zone, between the fifty-first parallel in the north and the forty-third in the south. Near the Atlantic coast, the influence of the ocean keeps temperatures moderately cool in summer and relatively warm in winter, but the Mediterranean Sea has little influence on French climate in general because of coastal mountains, the Maritime Alps, which block Mediterranean weather from moving inland. The exception is in the Rhone Valley, which lies between the Alps and the Massif Central, the low mountains in the center of France. Here Mediterranean climate is able to penetrate some distance.

Mediterranean France has less than fifty days of rain per year; the regions of Brittany and Normandy in the northwest have more than two hundred. Most of France has typical continental weather; cold air masses in winter and pleasant temperatures in summer. The weather plays an important part in daily life. Farmers and fishermen, of course, depend on good weather for their livelihood, and so do France's tourist centers—with cities along the coast, such as St. Tropez, Nice, and Cannes, counting on warm weather in summer, and ski resorts in the mountains, like Chamonix, Val d'Isère, and Super Bagnères, on abundant snow in winter.

Prehistoric Life

France was not always limited by its present natural borders. Twice in the past, the country's borders have extended to include most of Europe. Until 1940 France was a great colonial power, second only to Great Britain. During World War Two, it was reduced to half of its present size.

The Lauscaux paintings, found in caves in the Dordogne region, are over twenty thousand years old.

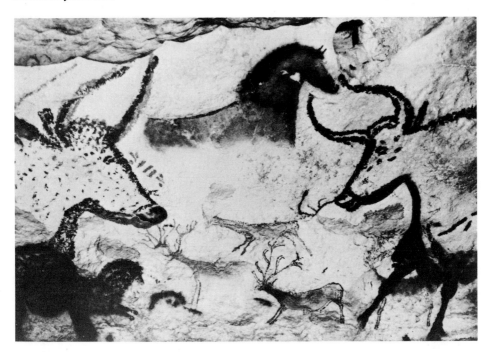

How was this country formed? Who were the first Frenchmen? Who were the rulers that had the greatest impact on the country's history? How did the present borders of France come about?

France is old. A very comprehensive record of the history of Western Europe has been found there, and the very earliest, vague remains date from one hundred thousand years ago, during the period when the great glaciers were carving out the troughlike valleys.

In 1940, near the town of Montignac in the Dordogne region, the Lascaux Cave was discovered. The cave walls were covered with fine paintings of animals, indicating that the Stone Age people who lived there more than twenty thousand years ago hunted reindeer, buffalo, and horses. Modern archaeologists have speculated that the paintings may have served as some sort of magic that was to bring success to the hunters who pursued these animals.

About ten thousand years ago, when the glaciers retreated, dense forests began to grow in France. Many of these forests have been cut down or thinned out, but they still cover more than one fifth of the total land area. During the centuries, the huge beams used for the cathedrals, châteaux, and great houses were cut there. Hunters frequented forests looking for game. Today, most woodland is protected from overcutting, and hunting is permitted only during certain seasons. Hunters go after rabbits, deer, pheasants, and other game.

Around 4000 B.C. an important Neolithic farming culture was established along the Mediterranean coast and up the Rhone Valley. Pottery shards, arrowheads, and ground stone axes have been found in Brittany, indicating that northwestern France was settled around 3000 B.C. Although no one really knows the exact purpose and age of the huge menhirs, or dolmens, located at Carnac and elsewhere in France, it is generally agreed that some were erected to mark common burial tombs.

The Birth of France

By 600 B.C., the country was occupied mostly by Celts, whom the Romans called Galli, or Gauls. These people never achieved complete political unity, and they were conquered by Julius Caesar in 58 B.C. Within the next eight years, the Romans conquered all the lands north of the Mediterranean—to the Rhine River in the northeast and the English Channel in the northwest, and the province of Gaul soon became an important part of the Roman Empire.

In the fifth century A.D., Gaul suffered a series of barbaric invasions. The Visigoths and the Vandals crossed Gaul and moved on into Spain; other tribes followed into Gaul. The most important of the invading tribes were the Franks, which were divided into two branches, the Salian in the north and the Ripuarian in the south. Clovis, the leader of the Salian Franks, in 486 overthrew the Roman general Syagrius and then defeated or stopped the other tribes that were threatening Gaul—the Alamanni, the Visigoths, and the Burgundians. He became a Christian, conquered most of Gaul, and united all the Franks under his rule. Clovis I is regarded as the founder of the Frankish state. His dynasty is called the Merovingian, after Meroveus, his grandfather.

Ideas of Grandeur, Heroism, Honor

The first hero French schoolchildren learn to revere is a man who is said to have stood up to Julius Caesar. General Vercingetorix was born around 72 B.C., and Caesar claimed he was chief of the Gallic tribes. He was young and a good orator. After having fought several successful battles against the Romans, Vercingetorix was surrounded on the hill of Alesia, about 160 miles southeast of Paris. There he was forced to surrender. Caesar brought him triumphantly to Rome, and after having been imprisoned for six years, Vercingetorix was executed.

In Caesar's writings, which are the only accounts we have, the general is depicted as a hero and Caesar's principal adversary in his campaigns; but some modern writers claim that Caesar exaggerated in order to augment the value of his victories. They say that Vercingetorix never should have permitted himself to be surrounded in the first place, that he let his cavalry charge too soon, and that, for a general, he was, all in all, a poor tactician.

Whatever the truth may be, Vercingetorix continues to be a hero to the French, who, in time of need, have an incredible ability to delve into their past and come up with heroes. Louis Napoleon, for example, had a commemorative statue of Vercingetorix built on the plateau of Mont

Auxois, as Alesia is called today. In the nineteenth century, having lost the territories of Alsace and Lorraine to the Germans, French historians built up Vercingetorix as a symbol of French unity. Alsace and Lorraine had to be recaptured at any price. Similarly, after the defeats of World War Two, General de Gaulle evoked the image of Vercingetorix as an early patriot. De Gaulle was searching for an example all Frenchmen would understand, and he distorted the facts. He wrote that the reason Vercingetorix surrendered "may have been so that this desperate homage to discipline might serve as an immortal lesson for his race." De Gaulle, in his usual flowery language, was attempting to make the French more aware of France as a nation, despite its humiliating defeat and occupation during World War Two.

Whether Vercingetorix was a good or bad general or a unifier of France is unimportant. What is important is the attitude the French adopt, from their first days in school, toward this hero. For many modern Frenchmen, Vercingetorix was a man who stood up against authority, an individualist. He was a man who was defeated and executed for his acts, but a man of valor. He never renounced his cause, he lived and died by the sword, an honorable and faithful soldier.

The Romanesque cathedral of Notre Dame in Le Puy in south-central France owes its unique appearance to Islamic influence.

Charles Martel and Christianity

Because it was the Frankish custom to divide the kingdom among all the king's sons, the Merovingians' power and authority grew steadily weaker as time went on. They have been described as the idle kings, for they relinquished their rule to magnates, and eventually to the so-called mayors of the palace, whose position was something like that of a prime minister.

The Carolingian family, which had produced some of the most capable mayors of the palace, grew in importance as the power of the Merovingians declined. Early in the eighth century, the Moors crossed the Pyrenees from Spain and invaded Gaul, and it was a Carolingian, Charles Martel who met and defeated them on the plain of Poitiers. If the Moors had won that battle, Gaul might well have fallen to the world of Islam, for the Moors had already conquered the Iberian Peninsula, and Charles Martel is generally credited with having saved France for Christianity.

He is remembered for another important reason. After the defeat of the Moors, Martel reorganized his military forces. Until that time soldiers were freemen, recruited as needed, and they fought on foot. After seeing the cavalry of the Arabs, Martel appropriated land and gave it to his vassals on the understanding that each was then obliged to keep a horse and be ready to go to war when needed. Many vassals became professional soldiers. The aristocracy throughout the kingdom imitated Martel's reform and began to build up private armies of vassals. This development had a profound effect on the social structure and gave the landed aristocracy both military and political power.

When Martel's son, Pepin the Short, who was deeply religious, succeeded him in 741, the contact with the papacy in Rome increased considerably. It was Pepin who finally put a stop to the nominal rule of the Merovingians. He deposed their last king and made himself king of the Franks. The dynasty of Clovis was at an end, and the new Carolingian dynasty was characterized by a fundamentally religious attitude. "From this time forward," writes historian Henri Pirenne, "the ideal of the king was not to be a Caesar, a potentate deriving his power and authority only from earthly sources; but to ensure that the divine

33

This statue of Charlemagne on his charger can be admired near the cathedral of Notre Dame in Paris.

precepts prevailed on earth and to govern in accordance with Christian morality; that is, in accordance with the church."

Charlemagne

What was lacking, however, to give true authority to the proclamations of the king was the official sanction of the church. The forces set in motion by Charles Martel, and even more so by Pepin the Short, were driven to their logical conclusion by Pepin's son, Carolus Magnus, or Charlemagne (Charles the Great). Early in Charles's reign, the power struggle between the eastern and the western branches of the church—the Byzantine Empire and Rome—still persisted. The Pope in Rome had given his support to the Frankish state. But this was a two-way street, for the state was made responsible for the safety of the church; Charlemagne had to subdue the Lombards, who had been threatening Rome for a number of years.

Having northern Italy in his power, Charles moved into Spain, where he defeated the Moors. Then, moving eastward, he fought the Slavs and the Avars, a Mongol tribe. But his most important enemy was the Saxons, who occupied a good part of Germany.

The Saxons were especially troublesome for Charlemagne because they held so tenaciously to their heathen beliefs. For the first time in Europe, there was an attempt to spread Christianity by force rather than by persuasion. Charlemagne demanded that the Saxons accept Christianity and become part of the Frankish state. Otherwise, their crime would be a double one: against the church and against the state which was governed by a king sanctioned by God. In the Saxon wars of 780 and 804, Charlemagne, acting in accordance with his allegiance to the church and his personal religious beliefs, massacred his adversary. With similar reasoning, nine hundred years later, Louis XIV was to persecute the Huguenots.

Political reasons, in addition to religious ones, motivated Charlemagne's extensive military activity. With his victory over the Saxons, Charlemagne brought the area now known as Germany not only into the Christian sphere of influence, but into the Frankish empire. All along the frontiers of his vast territory Charlemagne set up buffer states under military authority.

Under Charlemagne, religion became an essential factor of the political order—a fact that was to have profound consequences on the life of France and other European nations. To bind this church-state relationship even more closely, the papacy decided to reconstitute the Roman Empire. In that way, "the authority of the Pope and that of the Emperor, while remaining distinct from each other would nevertheless be as closely associated as the soul with the flesh in the human body."

On Christmas Day, in the year 800, Pope Leo III placed the crown on the head of Charlemagne, the king of the Franks. The pontiff declared Charlemagne emperor of the West and prostrated himself at Charles's feet.

The significance of this official joining of the church with the state should not be underestimated. Because of it, throughout the centuries, many projected solutions to the problems of France and other countries were measured in terms of whether they would be of benefit to the church and/or the state. For hundreds of years religious wars were fought. Protestants and other "nonbelievers" were persecuted. Some French kings were religiously oriented toward the papacy; under their reign Catholicism did well. Other kings appropriated church land; and in one way or another, the church retaliated. Thus, the church-state relationship formed and solidified during the time of Charlemagne played a profound role in France's future.

The Demise of the Empire

In administrative affairs, Emperor Charlemagne attempted many reforms. Latin became the spoken language. A small academy was formed in the palace in which sons of the aristocracy were instructed, and Charlemagne copied many of the administrative procedures found in the church organization. But because of its size, dangers from without, and lack of a cohesive organization, the empire was doomed to dissolution.

At Charlemagne's death the empire went to his son, Louis the Pious, whose three sons divided the vast lands among themselves. Francia Occidentalis (France) went to Charles the Bald, Francia Orientalis (Germany) to Louis the German, and Francia Media (the area extending from the Low Countries to Italy) to Emperor Lothair I.

During the next several centuries, the outlines of France changed often, and it was not until early in the eighteenth century, in the Treaty of Utrecht, that the "natural borders" of France were established. The Duchy of Lorraine was incorporated into France in 1766, and Corsica was ceded to France by Genoa in 1768. It was this transfer that made a French citizen out of Napoleon, a native of Corsica. During the Napoleonic wars the frontiers of France were once again stretched. They extended to the Elbe on the east and included Italy as far as Rome, much of Holland, and the Dalmatian coast. After Napoleon's defeat in the Battle of Waterloo, the Congress of Vienna in 1815 took away much of France's conquered territory. The frontiers reverted to what they had been in 1790. In 1860, the areas of the Savoy and Nice became part of France; and after the disastrous war of 1870 against Prussia, France lost much of the rich industrial areas of Alsace and Lorraine.

These often disputed territories were not returned until after the first World War, when France once again attained its "natural frontiers."

The Political Unity of France

The Carolingian dynasty was followed by that of the Capetians, after their first king, Hugh Capet, who came to the throne in 987, and whose male line continued uninterrupted for almost 350 years. At that time, most of France was divided into huge fiefdoms, such as Normandy, Burgundy, Aquitaine, Flanders, Anjou, Champagne, Brittany, and Toulouse, which surrounded a royal domain called the Île de France. This domain, which spread out from Paris, the administrative capital, had no outlet to the sea. In terms of wealth, the king's domain was poorer than any of the fiefdoms; but the king had certain traditional powers which had not yet been defined. The vassals or heads of the fiefdoms had sworn an oath of allegiance to the crown. They were obliged to perform military service when needed and to attend the king's councils. With the succession of each king by his son, the idea of the sovereignty of the king was gradually established. This was the first step toward a unification of France. Though the king was still devoid of real power,

The famous Bayeux tapestry depicts the Norman conquest of England in 1066. It is a coarse strip of linen 20 inches wide and 230 long and embroidered in eight colors.

Paris in the eleventh century was a city of great prestige and a growing rival to Rome. Paris was where the court was and where the principal schools of learning were, which were attached to the monasteries.

The coronation of the Duke of Normandy as king of England in 1066 posed a threat to Paris. The Capetian king realized that it was essential for France to establish a foreign policy and this necessitated the first alliances between the king of France and many of his vassals. In time, these alliances grew and with them the power and influence of the French king. By the twelfth century, as a result of important economic and social transformations, all northern French cities had sworn allegiance to the crown. King Philip Augustus was able to extract feudal dues from these cities, thus giving the monarchy "the indispensable instrument of all political power: financial resources," as the historian Henri Pirenne points out. Trade between the cities grew. Money was now minted. Philip Augustus established a treasury that could pay soldiers in times of war. Even more important, the treasury gave him the prerogative to hire and fire administrators, who were called bailiffs. Previous to this time these posts were handed down from generation to generation and the king did not have power of dismissal.

Whereas previous kings and emperors had governed through prestige obtained in wars or by appointment by the church, Philip Augustus was able to set up a permanent administration independent of religious authority. Thus, true power reverted to the king and the king alone. Philip Augustus can be regarded as the creator of monarchical power not only in France but throughout the Continent as well.

Further unification of France took place under succeeding monarchs. Gradually, the role of the king grew from that of simple protector of the rights of the crown to encompass such responsibilities as the maintenance of public order and the improvement of the condition of the people. Under Louis IX in the thirteenth century, "private wars were abolished, personal serfdom was suppressed on the royal domain, the judicial system was completed by providing for the right of appeal, and taxation was rendered more equitable," Henri Pirenne sums up. One result of these reforms was that the people began to revere the king as an ally in time of need, a person appointed by God, who could help them against the forces of injustice.

By now, France was the richest and most powerful kingdom in western Europe. It was geographically well situated; it had a population of fifteen million and had a robust political constitution. It was also the center of Western civilization. The French were enthusiastic participants in the Crusades. The code of chivalry was developed. Gothic art began to flourish, as did the *chansons de geste* (epic poems). French language, literature, and manners spread throughout Europe. Paris became the focal point of theological and philosophical studies in Western Christendom.

The Hundred Years' War and the House of Valois

Historians have searched in vain for that "vital necessity" that precipitated the Hundred Years' War. Neither England nor France was as yet a great commercial power; their economic aims never came into conflict. Thus, the war's cause was not a struggle for markets.

A French couple goes shopping under the old walls of Carcassonne.

The war's pretext was the claim, in 1337, of England's King Edward III to the French crown. When the three sons of Philip the Fair had died without leaving an heir, Philip of Valois, a nephew, was elected to be king of France. Edward's claim was through his mother Isabella, who was the daughter of Philip the Fair. But by now, French national sentiment and unity had grown too strong to accept an English king. When Edward found he was not welcome in France, he attacked, and once the war had broken out, neither side could give in without losing prestige. So the war went on and on for over a century, and only when both countries had become exhausted was it possible to establish a lasting truce.

Neither country really won the war. In the beginning, France had certain obvious advantages. The fighting took place on French soil. France was much richer than England, and its population was two or three times as numerous. But as time went on, the French kings were forced to contract debts that created important obligations on their part and thus weakened their overall power.

Early in the war the French were badly beaten at Crécy and at Poitiers. Taxation and discontent were high on both sides, and a temporary armistice—one of many—took place. After the terrible French defeat in the Battle of Agincourt in 1415, the French fiefdom of Normandy once again became British. (Normandy and three other fiefdoms had been temporarily under English rule during the twelfth century, as the result of a royal marriage.)

In 1422, both England's Henry V and France's Charles VI died, and a new crisis followed when Henry VI was proclaimed king of both France and England. The French people once more refused to recognize an Englishman as their king. They felt that their true king was the dauphin, the future Charles VII. But the problem was to convince him to assume his right to the throne and then to get him legally crowned.

Joan of Arc

Joan of Arc, the Maid of Orléans, was a farmer's daughter born in 1412 in Domrémy in the province of Lorraine. Extremely religious, she heard voices that commanded her to save France from the English invaders. In 1429, wearing armor and trousers—which shocked the church—Joan led a band of faithful men to Orléans. At Chinon she saw the dauphin and convinced him that his mission was to save France from the English. Given a detachment of soldiers to lead, Joan freed the city of Orléans, under siege by the English. She then marched on Paris, but was wounded at the Saint-Honoré gate. Shortly thereafter, she was betrayed and turned over to the English, was tried by the church, and in 1431 was burned at the stake as a witch. However, she had lived to see Charles VII consecrated king of France in the cathedral at Reims.

The importance of Joan of Arc for the French people cannot be overestimated. For hundreds of years the French have had a habit of adapting their heroes and heroines for immediate national purposes. Joan of Arc is the perfect example. Her fundamental religious motives have often been distorted. In 1803 Napoleon Bonaparte, who needed public support for his campaign against the English, had a monument of Joan erected at Orléans. When the territory of Lorraine was lost to the Germans in 1870, Joan became a symbol of vengeance—a person who had saved France during a time of crisis. And during World War One, historians claimed that Joan had been a great military tactician.

Millions of Frenchmen have died on the ramparts and in the trenches defending national causes. Many went off to war inspired from their first days in school by the image of the faithful virgin riding on a sturdy white horse. Today, the second Sunday in May is a national holiday: Joan of Arc Day. Thus, Joan of Arc continues to represent the national character of France in its purest form. She is the glory and honor of the country, and every enemy of France has to confront that symbol.

Fifteenth- and Sixteenth-Century France

Once the Hundred Years' War ended, economic conditions in France and the rest of Europe improved considerably. Trade and commerce grew along with industry. Even more important than the economic improvement was the intense intellectual development of the country. The sixteenth century was filled with optimism and a feeling that a new epoch was beginning. Rediscovery of the classics by the humanists as well as the development of printing, establishment of public libraries, and the enthusiasm for the ancient art of Greece were important developments of the period.

From 1494 until 1516 the French Kings Charles VIII, Louis XII, and Francis I went to war with Italy. France, however, won nothing of durable political value from these Italian adventures. What was of importance was the contact with the Renaissance. Francis was astonished by the highly developed Italian civilization, which was to have an important impact on French life.

Economic life in the sixteenth century was greatly influenced by the influx of gold and silver from the New World, the development of industry, monetary crises, rises in prices, the diminishing of the fortunes of the nobles, and the increased wealth of the bourgeoisie. The publishing industry developed in small workshops. The textile industry was already organized into larger establishments. Lyons became the center of cotton and silk weaving. Workers were poorly paid and lived in misery. But home workshops with looms also developed. In these, industrialists furnished the peasants with the raw materials—wool,

This statue of Francis I, one of France's most famous kings, decorates the main square of Cognac, his birthplace.

silk, or linen—and bought the finished product. Such rural home industries lasted in France until the nineteenth century.

Francis I, the Pleasure King

In order to finance their châteaux, the luxuries of their courts, and the "wars of magnificence"—adventurous expeditions, mostly to Italy—the kings were obliged to borrow money from rich bankers. In some cases this was never repaid. Francis I was the first French king to borrow money directly from the Notables, a group of powerful aristocrats. This was the beginning of France's public debt. Several thousand persons attended the king's sumptuous court, which became the center of the political and social life of the country. For those who wanted to get ahead, the court was the only answer. Sometimes the court was at Paris, but more often it moved to Saint-Germain, Fountainebleau, or the châteaux in the Loire Valley: Amboise, Blois, and Chambord. Wherever it was, the court conducted hunting parties, tournaments, balls, concerts, and theater productions.

As for the ruling power, this was centered in the hands of the king. Even though there were seven provincial parliaments, these were rarely convoked. Francis I's reign was marked by progress in legislation, particularly in law, which was no longer written in Latin but in French. He created customs taxes, the *taille,* or tax on the common people, and taxes on certain produce. Not having sufficient money, the government sold public offices—often superfluous posts—a ruinous practice which lasted until the Revolution of 1789.

Despite the excesses of Francis I and Henry II, his successor, the importance of Lyons textiles and printing grew, and the administrative importance of Paris could no longer be disputed. The population of France also increased. Most of the wars took place outside the country's frontiers; the peasants, if they were not recruited into the army, were relatively secure.

Religious Persecutions

From the first, Francis I and Henry II had fought the Huguenots, as the Calvinist Protestants in France were called. Religious persecution was the order of the day, but in spite of it many nobles abandoned their Catholic faith for the new teachings. Soon the country was split into two groups, and although the church instituted certain reforms and made attempts at unifying the population, the cruel French Wars of Religion broke out in 1562, which were to last for almost forty years. Catholics were supported by the king of Spain; Protestants, by the queen of England. In 1572, the massacre of Saint Bartholomew's Day took place, in which hundreds of Huguenots were slaughtered.

Henry IV

Despite the terrible massacre, the Protestants had gained certain advantages during the struggle, and Henry III, the last Valois king, chose as his successor Henry of Navarre, a Protestant who had been one of the Huguenot leaders. Another Henry, Henri de Guise, opposed this choice, and the War of the Three Henrys broke out, from which Henry of Navarre emerged as the victor. As king of France, however, Henry decided to become a Catholic, saying, "Paris is well worth a Mass."

Henry IV, who was the first of the Bourbons, finally brought some order into the chaos. He restored peace in the land with the Edict of Nantes in 1598, which established freedom of religion in France and gave certain political rights to the Huguenots as well. He reestablished the authority of the monarchy and put the country on a sound economic footing. Maximilien de Béthune, Duke of Sully, his brilliant finance minister, increased indirect taxes, refused sums demanded by the court, reduced the public debt, and increased the country's gold reserves. He realized that France could become one of the most important agricultural countries in Europe, saying, "Pasture land and plowing are the two breasts by which France is nourished. . . ."

For the first time, government protection of the common man became a reality as Sully set about defending the rights of the peasants. It was forbidden for noblemen to hunt in the vineyards or grain fields; taxes were diminished; and it was an offense to seize the animals of a peasant.

La Rochelle on the Bay of Biscay, south of Nantes, was one of the strongest Protestant cities in sixteenth-century France. Today, the city of 70,000 is known mainly for its fishing fleet and protected yacht harbor.

With reforms in government and the encouraging of industry, in ten years the country recovered from the damages caused by the wars. Henry IV was assassinated in 1610 because of his liberal views toward the Huguenots; but he is regarded as the most popular ruler France ever had.

Cardinal Richelieu

Louis XIII, Henry's son, was only nine years old when he became king, and religious and foreign wars began again. When Louis finally was able to extricate himself from the influence of his mother, Marie de Médicis, who had been regent, he put the government into the hands of Cardinal Richelieu, giving him complete control over the government. Richelieu centralized royal authority, refusing to give the parliaments

Louis XIV, le Roi Soleil.

the right to discuss state affairs. For the first time in France, propaganda was used to justify government actions; this appeared in France's first newspaper, *La Gazette,* published in 1631. Richelieu strengthened France's army and navy and engaged in warfare against the Hapsburg Empire. He took away some of the rights granted to the Huguenots in the Edict of Nantes, and when he died in 1642 he was hated by all and trusted only by the king.

Le Roi Soleil

If you ask the average Frenchman who, during the thousand years of monarchy in France, was the greatest of French kings, the likelihood is that he will reply Louis XIV, *le Roi Soleil,* or the Sun King. And

46

if you ask why, he may say, "He lived in great splendor. He surrounded himself with beautiful things. He built Versailles." Or, if you are talking to a well-educated person, he may say, "Louis XIV was a great king because his reign enriched arts and letters; he furthered great playwrights like Racine and Molière, poets like La Fontaine and Boileau, artists like Poussin, Le Lorrain, Mansart, and Puget."

Louis XIV chose the sun as his emblem, and for French people today the Sun King's reign still symbolizes dazzling splendor. During the seventy-two years of his rule he was personally interested in everything that went on in his kingdom. In Louis's case, as in that of Francis I, this also included seeking glory through war and imposing on other countries the superiority of France.

Louis XIV was an extraordinary monarch. He had a mania for detail and appointed highly capable men to handle the country's administration. Finance Minister Jean-Baptiste Colbert put twelve thousand men

The symbol of Louis XIV was the sun. Motifs such as this one from a huge urn can be found throughout Versailles, where the king held court.

to work to build the Canal du Midi, which still connects the city of Toulouse with the Mediterranean. He set up trading companies and sub-sidized state industries, like the Gobelins tapestry works, which are still in existence. He also published an illustrated encyclopedia of arts and crafts, which at the time was a considerable achievement. Besides Colbert, other capable men were appointed to run the army and see to the fortifications of the country.

Despite the valiant efforts of the talented Colbert, the first great French economist, at the end of Louis XIV's rule France was in financial ruin. Mainly responsible were the wars with Spain and Holland; but also at fault were the agreements that Louis had made with the wealthy nobles of France. Later kings and their subjects had to pay heavily; and historians have pointed out that many of the seeds of the French Revolution were planted during the drive for glory and grandeur of the Sun King.

It is difficult to understand today why so many of the French people still admire Louis XIV. During his reign, the country was often engaged in "glorious wars" that exhausted it; the decision to revoke the Edict of Nantes led to religious persecution, the exodus of thousands of Protestants, and the loss to France of an incalculably valuable middle-class group; and the taxation of the common people was increased until it became almost unbearable. At the time of his death in 1715, worship of the king had taken the place of criticism of his acts, the economy was in a shambles, and Louis XIV had brought the French much closer to revolution.

What then is the Sun King's great attraction? The Palace of Ver-sailles and the artistic and literary achievements that came out of his court are one answer. But for many people what Louis XIV repre-sented most of all was style, just as General de Gaulle, more than two hundred years later, represented grandeur. There was something awe-inspiring about Louis, who fervently believed that he had been chosen by God; and, as we have seen, the French, perhaps more than other people, need heroes and heroines. They forget easily the terrible mistakes this monarch made, but they remember Versailles and the lavish court. This is part of the flair of the French—their love for the externals, for appearance, glory, grandeur, and all the show. Unfortunately, throughout French history, these externals sometimes be came more important than the realities.

The Clergy, Nobles, and the Third Estate

Although the reigns of Francis I, Henry IV, and Louis XIV were marked by many cultural and some economic advances, by the middle of the eighteenth century a profound inequality had grown up between the three classes, or estates, of society and even within each class itself. The three estates—clergy, nobles, and Third Estate—were not treated equally under the law and under the system of taxation. Privileges obtained through birth or tradition, and influence through intrigue were the guidelines to success; and, as we shall see, despite the French Revolution, the class structure—and all that it means— has filtered down into the current life of France.

The First Estate at the time of Louis XIV consisted of about 130,000 clergy, members of the monastic orders, and of the aristocracy. The clergy had permanent representatives living at Versailles and had influence over the king. They were not a real social class, but a professional category enjoying certain social privileges, such as the right to impose a tax on agricultural produce, and to maintain a court to judge religious offenses. They lived off revenues obtained from huge domains which were rented out. In fact, the church was the largest landlord in the kingdom. It paid low taxes and ran and supported certain schools.

Another group in the First Estate were the notables, or court aristocracy. They had lost all of their political power when, during 1648–1653, they had revolted against royal absolutism. This revolt was called the Fronde, and because of it Louis XIV appointed almost all his officials from the Third Estate Bourgeoisie.

The Second Estate consisted of about 400,000 hereditary nobles and the *noblesse de robe,* the nobility of the cloth—those persons who had bought government posts or had obtained their titles through royal decree. The nobles, like the clergy, had important social and tax privileges. Some lived in Paris, but by far the larger part lived as gentle-

Bringing the cow in for milking is a daily occupation in the French countryside. This farmhouse and outbuildings are made of stone, with peaked shingle- or slate-covered roofs.

men farmers on provincial estates. The nobles were the only class of people who were appointed military commanders, diplomats, and officials of the church by most of the monarchs.

By 1760 the population of France had grown to about 22 million people, of whom nine out of ten lived on farms or in small villages. The bulk of the Third Estate consisted of free peasants, about half of whom owned some land. The others were tenants, sharecroppers, or day laborers who worked either for the nobles or for the bourgeoisie, a group of rich merchants, bankers, tax collectors, professional men, and shopkeepers. Under Louis XIV, the bourgeoisie played a crucial role. From among them the king chose his administrators, judges, the *intendants* (provincial governors), members of his various councils, the state secretaries, and his ministers. Already in the society of the seventeenth

50

and eighteenth centuries there were clear advantages to being a government employee.

The bourgeoisie had become very restless by 1760. Over the years their appetite to share some of the privileges of the aristocratic classes had been heightened. They wanted to move up the ladder, but their progress, after the death of Louis XIV, was blocked by the aristocrats who had obtained a monopoly on the high offices. And so the bourgeoisie section of the Third Estate became the most fertile breeding ground for the Revolution.

Artisans and Laborers

Still lower on the social scale were the artisans, most of whom lived in the cities. As in the Middle Ages, all work was done by hand, and the only source of extra power was water. In most of the workshops a *patron,* or boss, was surrounded by two or three apprentices, and since these shops were inherited by the patrons' sons it was practically impossible for an apprentice to improve his lot. This was the origin of the distinction between the *patron* and his workers, still present in current French life.

In order to secure work for themselves when they traveled from one region to another, skilled workers formed secret societies called *compagnonnages.* Though prohibited, as were all associations not controlled by the monarchy, they were probably the beginnings of the French labor unions.

The Great Revolution and Nineteenth-Century France

> The French want to be equal while free, and if they cannot obtain that they want to be equal in slavery.—ALEXIS DE TOCQUEVILLE

Prerevolutionary France

Under the reigns of Louis XV and Louis XVI, conditions in France went from bad to worse. This was mainly due to the fact that the kings had little real interest in what happened in the kingdom. They were bored, timid, lazy, and indifferent. More and more, the government was run by the king's ministers, without supervision by the king himself. The public, which in the past had esteemed its monarchs, gradually turned against them. The Paris and provincial parliaments insisted on more and more control of the government. They stirred up the people, who began to talk of republican government and basic reform. By the time of the death of Louis XV in 1774, the prestige of the monarchy had dwindled, and a spirit of reform and revolution had grown in its place. This revolutionary climate was further aided by Louis XVI. Slow-witted and dull, Louis had only one passion: hunting. His queen, the frivolous, extravagant, and indiscreet Marie Antoinette, of Austria, was no help to him either. The times required an extremely strong monarch to stand up to the wealthy nobles and

Georges-Jacques Danton, after whom this café in the Latin Quarter of Paris is named, was one of the principal figures of the French Revolution. He was beheaded on orders from Robespierre in 1794.

François Marie de Voltaire was one of the most brilliant philosophers and authors of France during the eighteenth century.

clergy who made up the court and were bleeding it dry. Louis XVI was not that man.

The revolutionary climate became more intense when philosophers like Montesquieu, Voltaire, Diderot, and Rousseau took up the themes of revolution first voiced by the English philosophers. They attacked religion for its intolerances and despotism and demanded equality and liberty for all, public schooling organized and supported by the state, and the abolition of many of the institutions of the old regime. In certain European countries similar reforms were already under way.

The American Revolution eventually had a strong impact on the French people. General Lafayette enthusiastically came to aid the American cause, and six thousand men, as well as guns and ammunition, were sent to support the Colonists against the British. The war was a chance for the French to take revenge against their traditional enemy. But contact with the American struggle for independence made discussion of revolution respectable and fashionable in France

54

among all classes. It was one of those historic events that broke through class lines.

In the last quarter of the eighteenth century, a few piecemeal reforms were instituted; but "a great humanitarian spirit that had been centuries in the growing" could not be satisfied by establishing norms for the width of French roads or installing water in Parisian homes instead of having it carried from public fountains.

The Revolt of the Privileged Classes

The second major effect that the American Revolution had on France was that it put the country into bankruptcy—and this increased the chances of revolt. During the crucial 1777 to 1788 period, French finances were in the hands of the ambitious banker and minister Jacques Necker. A clever politician, he managed for years to keep public opinion on his side. But during his tenure of office, the royal debt increased fivefold, and he was as incapable of instituting meaningful reforms as the other finance ministers. Failure to collect taxes further increased the danger to the monarchy, and on top of everything else the loyalty of the army also began to be in doubt.

Since the middle of the eighteenth century, the provincial and Paris parliaments had grown in importance. These parliaments were made up of members of the nobility and clergy. Gradually, they began to think of themselves as the intermediaries between the king and the people. Many of their declarations reflected the ideas of the French revolutionary philosophers, and they violently attacked the king's ministers. By 1787 the parliamentarians were so popular that it seemed as if they could dictate their will to the king. They demanded the summoning of the States-General—elected representatives of the three groups of French society. The monarchy dismissed the parliaments, and the latter retaliated by organizing riots. They were supported by the church and the nobility who wanted to reestablish a strong provincial government able to defend their tax privileges, financial advantages, and landholdings. The situation was extremely serious. The royal coffers were empty, several ministers resigned, and open revolt broke out in the country.

Victory of the Third Estate

The king agreed to the convening of the States-General, or National Assembly. The nobles and clergy in the parliament wanted that body to be composed as it had been in 1614, the last time it had met. At that time the Third Estate was outnumbered two to one. However, the Third Estate had grown in importance, and, as the largest group in France, it did not want to be a minority in the National Assembly. Hundreds of pamphlets attacking the privileged classes were distributed and fanned the tension between the classes. "The Third Estate, which had been faithfully seconding the struggle of the privileged classes against royal despotism, suddenly discovered that its supposed allies were its enemies," wrote the English historian Alfred Cobban. When the king, again led by Necker, supported the claims of the Third Estate for doubling its representation in the States-General, he became popular once more. For the moment he had returned to the side of the people.

The French Revolution, as Robespierre pointed out, was triggered not by the common people or the Third Estate bourgeoise but by the nobles, the clergy, and the rich. Once the Revolution got under way, however, the Third Estate began to demand power. When that happened the privileged classes wished to stop the Revolution, but it was too late.

The convening of the States-General meant the end of what remained of absolute monarchy in France. In effect, the king had been forced to relinquish the authority of government to an elected assembly.

What drove the people from constitutional attempts at reforming government to revolution was the cost of food, particularly bread. Bread is the staff of life to the French and has played an important role in the country's political history. The people like it and eat a lot of it. If the price rises by as little as one cent, the chances of revolt are immeasurably increased. That was the case just before the outbreak of the French Revolution. The grain harvest of 1788 had been disastrous, and by 1789 bread prices had risen to new heights. Bread and grain riots swept the country. Unemployment had risen to about 50 percent. People were hungry, and, when told they had no bread, Marie An-

Irate Parisians storm the Bastille on July 14, 1789.

toinette was reported to have replied, "Let them eat cake." What aggravated the situation still further was that hunger and political agitation coincided. The masses of people, with half-empty stomachs, were open to the many revolutionary ideas of the period.

The States-General met on May 5, 1789. The representatives of the Third Estate were extremely disappointed when the king shifted his support to the side of the privileged classes. However, some liberal nobles and clergy supported the claims of the Third Estate, and on June 27 the king shifted ground once again. He issued instructions for the remainder of the clergy and the nobility to back the Third Estate. It was a complete turnabout, the reasons for which have never been known.

But the fury of the mobs had been set loose. What had up to that moment been a struggle of one segment of the population for more power turned into a civil war. Customs posts were destroyed by riots in Paris, and agitation existed in every quarter. Troops were called out, and the mobs grew in size and violence. Arms were sought. Mobs concentrated on the Bastille, the fortress where it was said hundreds of state prisoners were in jail. The Bastille was stormed, and the massacres began. Many of its defenders were beheaded and their heads carried around the city on pikes. The fall of the Bastille became a symbol of the end of the king's power, and Bastille Day—July 14—has been a national holiday ever since. As fear spread throughout Paris, many of the privileged classes fled for their lives to foreign countries. They were to remain there for decades, intriguing and hoping for a return to the old status quo. Meanwhile, the Third Estate was left with a revolution on its hands.

Ten Years of Revolt

The American Revolution took place in a new land, far from the mother country. Its cause was limited to the infringement of certain rights. The French Revolution, on the other hand, occurred on home soil and shook the thousand-year-old foundations of the French nation. In some respects, the effects of this terrible struggle can still be found in current French life. And, although there had been philosophies of revolution, poverty, a government practically in bankruptcy, propaganda, and rebellious speeches by the hundreds, the fact was that the people had had no experience in governing themselves. The monarchy had its grip on the government until the last possible moment, and the people were not prepared for the coming power. So it was that the French Revolution was a shock for the Third Estate bourgeoisie. Forces had been released that were hard to control, and situations had to be dealt with on a day-to-day basis. With the exodus of the aristocracy and a weak king residing in the palace of Versailles, a power vacuum had been created. Who was to fill that vacuum, and how? The next decade was to see a scramble for power on a scale unknown in European history.

In some provincial towns, revolutionary committees and communal councils simply took over the government; in others, agreements were reached with the old authorities. Rural unrest was strong and up-risings were frequent. It was practically impossible to control the peasantry. They refused to pay rent to the landowners; they burned down the homes of the nobles and pillaged whatever they could. In Paris, control over the city was temporarily gained by using the national guard and newly installed city authorities.

In August 1789, the States-General turned itself into a Constituent Assembly and drew up the French Declaration of Rights. That Declaration stated that men were free and equal. Its object was "to abolish distinctions based on privilege." People had the "natural, inalienable, sacred, and inviolable right to own property." There were provisions for freedom from arbitrary arrest; freedom of opinions, including religion; and freedom from taxation without consent. In addition, the

The Tuileries Gardens.

Declaration created a representative assembly, and it was stated that "the source of all sovereignty resides essentially in the nation." This clause was directed mainly against church influence.

The French Declaration of Rights was lofty in its principles and important in its influence on foreign countries like America and Scandinavia; but in practice the first written French constitution was violated almost immediately. During the ten years of Revolution, three different constitutions were voted, and every French regime since that time has interpreted the constitution to suit its particular needs.

More practical things remained to be done. France was divided into eighty-three *départements*. The power to appoint their own officials was granted to the communal councils. This system is similar to that which exists today.

Meanwhile, unrest was still rampant. In October 1789, a mob of twenty thousand hungry Parisians forced Louis XVI and the queen to leave the palace of Versailles and live in the Tuileries Palace in Paris. Throughout the country, revolutionary clubs were formed, and revolutionary leaders and profiteers emerged. Their aims were the exploitation of popular discontent, stirring up the mobs against the court aristocrats, the clergy, and the nobles. In addition, domestic and foreign agitators and journalists played a strategic role. Propaganda took on an importance never known before.

The Fall of the Constitutional Monarchy

Once the new French constitution had been passed in 1791 the Assembly was dissolved and a constitutional monarchy set up. This failed despite the desire on the part of the new Legislative Assembly to make it work; there were so many different factions in France struggling to take up the reins of power. Into the breach had rushed the ambitious men of the time: Mirabeau, Robespierre, Danton, and many others.

Partially to maintain the revolutionary fervor, France declared war on Prussia, a war for which the country was unprepared. Economic difficulties increased, and the work of domestic and foreign agitators brought about another revolution in 1792. The power of the Legislative Assembly was diminished, and a National Convention, elected by "universal suffrage"—actually less than 10 percent of the people voted —took its place. The Convention almost immediately reflected the dissension that had existed in the Legislative Assembly. Ranged on one side were the Girondists (after the *département* of Gironde, where their leaders came from). They were also called Brissotins, after one of their leaders. Allied with the Girondists were the Rolandists, also named after a revolutionary leader. Opposing them were the Jacobins from Paris, who were so called because they used to meet in an old Jacobin convent. Because of the seats they occupied high up at the back of the hall, the Jacobins became known as the Mountain. They were led by Robespierre. Most of the Convention deputies were lower down in the orchestra and were called the Plain. One of the first acts of the Convention was the abolition of the monarchy. King Louis XVI, who had been but a puppet and had been proved guilty of treason, was sentenced to death by a vote of 380 to 310. He was guillotined on January 21, 1793.

Meanwhile, the war against the Prussians went on. As the latter advanced on Paris, riots broke out in the city. Surprisingly, the Prussians were defeated at Valmy. The war having been a success, the French decided to attack their traditional enemy, Great Britain. Patriotic fervor was so strong in the country that the government also declared war on Holland and Spain. War, in a way, had become the element that was needed to channel and give release to the revolutionary patriotism so strong among the French masses. The French armies numbered 850,000, even though in some parts of the country there were outbreaks against conscription. Ten years later many of the successful generals were to become the marshals of Napoleon's army. Despite the large numbers of conscripts in the army, food riots, murders, and summary executions by the guillotine continued. As the historian Alfred Cobban wrote:

> The guillotine cut a swathe through the ranks of counterrevolutionaries and revolutionaries alike. Marie-Antoinette, after a trial in which all the indecent slanders of her enemies of the old court

were dragged up to discredit her, was executed in October, a tragic figure, sketched on her last journey, all her beauty gone, by the bitter pen of David. Brissot, Vergniaud, and twenty-nine of those arrested with them, their mouths silenced at their trial by a decree of the Convention, died, sacrificial victims on the altar of the republic they had striven to achieve. . . . The Duke of Orleans, unworthy Philippe-Égalité, mounted the steps of the guillotine instead of the throne and died with more dignity than he had lived. Mme. du Barry perished shrieking her head off, and Élisabeth, sister to the dead king, with religious devotion. Military leaders who had been defeated were guillotined to encourage the others. . . . 'Les dieux ont soif,' [the Gods are thirsty] cried Camille Desmoulins, and they cared little whose blood was poured out for their libation.

A powerful Committee of Public Safety was set up by the government in 1793 in order to strengthen its position in Paris and the provinces. This Committee, which operated during the most critical year of the Revolution, from July 1793 to June 1794, became the executive arm of the government. The Convention backed its actions. Capable and ruthless men like Robespierre, Billaud-Varenne, and Robert Lindet were among its leaders. They suppressed the opposition because the situation demanded unity. France was at war with most of Europe, and Paris was at war with much of France. Economic factors played into the hands of the most extreme revolutionaries. By the end of 1793 the Committee had achieved some control over the situation, through executions and terror. The war went well, and this strengthened its hand. The Committee controlled the press and propaganda; but when Robespierre himself demanded still more police powers he was sent to the guillotine.

Riots and anarchy continued in 1795. People cried: "Bread and the Constitution of 1793!" The Convention, desiring power, reduced the authority of the Committee of Public Safety. The Directory, a group of *nouveaux riches,* took over, and riots broke out in Paris once again. These were only brought to a halt in September 1797, when the army marched into the city. Behind them was the shadow of Napoleon, who had been in command of the army in Italy and had led an unsuccessful campaign in Egypt.

Results of the French Revolution

Someone has remarked that important changes in France traditionally occur not through legislation but in times of crises. Change, however, can bring about reforms or reaction, an improvement in the living standards of the masses or a favoring of special classes. Throughout the ten years of revolutionary turmoil, the monarchy lost all its prestige and power. King Louis XVI was no longer referred to as king of France but as king of the French. This was an important distinction because it removed from the monarchy the aura of divine right which had been established at the time of Charlemagne. In the last years of the French monarchy, the king was relegated to serving the people, if only symbolically. Still another important theme of the Revolution was its opposition to the clergy. Attacks on religion and the church were to continue throughout the nineteenth and twentieth centuries. Until the time of the Revolution, church property had been put into a separate category from other property; but during the decade of terror it was sold in order to help finance provincial and Paris governments and to satisfy the discontent of farmers and peasants. Alfred Cobban remarked, "That it was to be the first step in the secularization of the state and the commencement of a still unfinished war between the church and the Revolution hardly anyone guessed."

The Revolution also spelled the end to certain traditions in French life. The privileges of the clergy and aristocracy were abolished or sharply curtailed, and power passed into the hands of the bourgeoisie. Some land was distributed to the peasants, but once that was done, that group played no further part in the conflict. By the end of the century, the people wanted to restore stability at any price. Meaningful reforms went by the board, and the conservative pattern of French life was set, to carry its traditions into the nineteenth and twentieth centuries.

One positive result of the Revolution was that it freed the individual from the feudalism of the Middle Ages. This did not mean that

democracy had been achieved; it simply meant that the individual, whatever his class, could have some effect on his country's destiny, and he was no longer an anonymous being. In 1800 this was still but an idea. The next century and a half were to witness the slow emergence of individual rights.

From the French Revolution to modern times, France has participated in, and, in some cases, provoked nine major wars, not to mention the colonial conquests and the colonial wars of independence, most recently in Indo-China and Algeria. Through these terrible series of wars, certain French attitudes toward authority and their fellowmen inevitably developed. One of the most important of these attitudes is the people's distrust of government, of reform, or of extremists—be they French or foreign. These attitudes can be traced back to the Revolution when the bourgeoisie inherited power from the aristocracy.

Napoleon Bonaparte

Napoleon had more influence over French life than any other Frenchman. Born in Ajaccio, Corsica, in 1769, he was a great general and leader of men. On the battlefield his chief virtue was his ability to improvise. The blitzkrieg attack and the loyalty of his *grognards*—grumblers, as Napoleon's soldiers were called—were his principal weapons. His military campaigns, however, are amply described in history books; what concerns us here is Napoleon's profound contributions to nineteenth- and twentieth-century France.

In 1799, Napoleon entered Paris as a military hero. After a *coup d'état* he was elected First Consul of France; in 1802 he became Consul for life; and in 1804 he was crowned emperor with the blessing of the Pope. This gave him complete dictatorial powers. He was realistic, had great executive capacities, a ruthless strength of will, tremendous energy, and a powerful memory. He used propaganda effectively, and through personal charm and favors, he won over key persons without whose support he could not have ruled France for long. But he had many enemies who plotted against him, and assassination attempts were frequent.

Besides the attainment of personal glory, Napoleon wanted to found a dynasty. As First Consul he kept intact the legislative bodies which had grown out of the Revolution, but their function was to rubber-stamp what the emperor proclaimed. He reorganized the ministries and created a minister of police, so important in a dictatorial state. Napoleon consulted his ministers from time to time and gave them orders, which they were obliged, for fear of their lives, to carry out.

He instituted the office of Consul of State, or Consulate, which was composed of experts from many of the different factions in French political life. Their purpose was to draw up laws and administrative regulations. At the same time, they were a check on the ministries. The most important act of the Consulate was the creation of a system of administrative laws. These laws became the cornerstone of French government and were among the most powerful instruments of bureaucratic control that the Western world had known since the Roman Empire.

With the central government organized, Napoleon turned to the provincial ones. During the Revolution, local governments had been elected and the work in the provinces was performed by councils. Napoleon abandoned local elections, limited the role of the councils, and put each *département* under the authority of a *préfect* appointed by Paris. The *préfecture,* an office that still exists today, served as liaison between the central and the local government. It was the *préfect*'s job to rule his *département* and serve Napoleon's purposes.

Napoleon appointed a group of prominent lawyers and gave them five months to draw up a uniform legal code, which was adopted in 1804 and came to be known as the Code Napoléon. It reduced the legal status of women, tightened marriage and divorce laws, and declared the supremacy of the father in the family structure. Its more than two thousand articles touched on almost every aspect of French life. In the twentieth century some of the Code Napoléon was changed; but its purpose remains clear: Organize family life, and all else in society, in such a way as to back the state, or rather Napoleon's purposes. Although there were serious defects in the Code, it did maintain many of the gains of the Revolution, such as equality before the law, religious toleration, and abolition of privileges. The Code had a great effect not only on French life but on the legal codes of many other European countries as well.

The administration removed the system of local control over taxation and placed it in the hands of the central government. The wealthy used all means at hand to avoid paying taxes for the privilege of being governed. Thus a pattern for hiding material wealth from the tax collectors was set. Some indirect taxes were established, and Napoleon is generally given credit for the establishment of the Bank of France.

The façade of the Strasbourg Cathedral, begun in 1277 by Erwin of Steinbach, is a model of composition; the doorways and the famous angel pillar rank among the masterpieces of Gothic art.

The Religious Settlement

On the one hand, the Pope wanted to see Catholicism once again accepted as the official religion of France; on the other hand, Napoleon needed the blessing of the Pope, as did Charlemagne before him, to be crowned emperor. The dictator also realized that a religious settlement would serve his purposes. During the Revolution, a certain revival of religious sentiment had taken place, probably because of the terrible violence set loose. Napoleon wanted to tap this feeling in order to give himself more control over the people. "The people," he is alleged to have said, "must have a religion, and that religion must be in the hands of the government."

The Concordat was announced in 1802. In this document, as historian Cobban points out, the Vatican "agreed to the institution of a new episcopate which should contain a proportion of bishops from the Constitutional Church, recognized the alienation of Church lands as permanent, and accepted the payment of clerical salaries by the state. Catholicism was described as 'the religion of the great majority of citizens,' and its practice was to be free and public so long as it conformed to such police regulations as were required by public order." The Concordat was a great victory for Napoleon, who proceeded to use the clergy to celebrate his military triumphs. The clergy delivered patriotic sermons, helped to overcome the reluctance of the people toward conscription in the army, and performed many other services.

During the prerevolutionary monarchies, education had been controlled by the church. Napoleon set about organizing a state school system which was adopted in 1808. *Lycées,* or high schools, were established, along with specialized schools for law, medicine, pharmacy, and military history and tactics. A special school called the *École Normale* was to provide the state with technical experts and top administrators. The purpose of the secondary schools was to provide the state with minor officials. These schools, as well as the primary institutions, were directed by city governments or, in the case of private schools, run by individuals. In charge of the school system was a director located in Paris.

Under Napoleon's fifteen-year rule (from 1799 to 1804 as First Consul, and from 1804 to 1814 as emperor), newspapers served the government or disappeared, books were censored, the theater was controlled by the police, and art and literature languished. Napoleon's innovations—the Consulate, the code of civil law, the educational system, the Legion of Honor medal for military heroes—became

68

part of French life. These institutions have had more effect on the French people of today than the many battles Napoleon won and lost.

Nineteenth-Century France

The ghost of Napoleon haunted the nineteenth century. During this period France shifted back and forth between monarchy, empire, and republic. When, after the fall of Napoleon, King Louis XVIII and his successor, Charles X, took over, their power was limited by the new aristocracy. In addition, the power of both the king and the nobles was now limited by a chamber of deputies, and the wealthy had to take into account the interests of the rising middle class. In many ways, though, France in the nineteenth century was very similar to France in the eighteenth century. Napoleon as emperor had taken the place of the king; the court was at Saint-Cloud instead of at Versailles. Attached to it were fewer nobles. There was a parliament, but it lacked the independence of the parliaments during the *ancien régime*. The financial men were there in number and exercised considerable political and social power. The church had again come to terms with the state and, to increase its influence, was doing all it could to thwart national policies and reforms. Paris had grown in size and had been rebuilt. The poorer classes lived on the outskirts, and the city had become more important as a center of administration, government, art, letters, and finance. By 1870 the cities had developed considerably, and their population had increased to over 20 million.

In the provinces some industrialization had taken place. The railroad, constructed during the reign of Louis Napoleon, was the same as it had been a century earlier. Instead of the *intendants* who administered the *généralités* there were now *préfects* who ruled the *départements*. For the ordinary man the pattern of daily life had changed little; for the peasantry, life had changed hardly at all.

The Industrial Revolution had taken hold in many European countries, but in France it had hardly begun. Landlords and stockbrokers dominated the upper classes and were extremely conservative. France had not yet become what many have contemptuously called

"Take Versailles, add on Antwerp, and you will have Bordeaux," said Victor Hugo, who was impressed by the eighteenth-century architecture and the Gironde River which winds through the city.

England: "the nation of shopkeepers." France was still basically rural, and those few peasants who had become landowners were suspicious of any changes that might alter their newly gained status. Preservation of their economic wealth was the essential thing for them. Moral justification for wealth was dealt out by the church. The government's administrative structure had been fixed by Napoleon. Society was reactionary, conservative, and static. Political disturbances occasionally tore at the structure, but they were due to the loose ends that the Revolution had left, and the existence of vital issues the new administrative system could not cope with. Occasional revolutions broke out when political and economic crises coincided. This happened in 1821, 1830, 1831, 1848, and 1870. The major effect of these uprisings was to remove from power some of the administrative personnel and, at the same time, to reduce to obscurity some of France's most able civil servants.

France in the nineteenth century was materialistic, unstable, and lacking in ideology. The country was ruled by the propertied classes; elections were almost always controlled by the simple measure of making the right to vote contingent on certain conditions. Religious schism was a common theme, used to help the propertied classes maintain their hold over the rest of the population.

It was not until the final thirty years of the century that the Industrial Revolution began to have an effect on French life. The population shift to the cities began and brought with it many of the joys and problems of modern society.

The Emergence of French Democracy and Charles de Gaulle

Take the loftiest possible position—it is inevitably the least crowded.
—CHARLES DE GAULLE

The first Republic of France lasted from 1792 to 1795. The constitution of the Second Republic and the term of Louis Napoleon, Bonaparte's nephew, as President lasted from 1848 until 1852. After that an empire was set up, and Louis Napoleon became emperor. Late in Louis Napoleon's reign, however, a movement was started to abolish the empire once and for all and begin real republican government. Louis Napoleon was forced to restore parliamentary government in 1869, and in 1875 the Third Republic constitution was voted. Under that constitution the following institutions were established: two houses of parliament, one called the National Assembly, to be elected directly by the people, and the other called the Senate, with members indirectly elected; the president of France, to be elected by the two houses of parliament; and a premier, to lead the government in power and appoint the other ministers.

This was the general structure of government until the 1960's. From the beginning, modern French governments had trouble. There were so many different political parties and pressure groups, all with varying interests, that it was practically impossible for them to reach lasting

General de Gaulle leaving the Arc de Triomphe and marching down the Champs Élysées flanked by members of the resistance on Liberation Day in Paris, August 25, 1944.

73

agreements. Added to that was the French distrust of authority. After all, there had been so many governments! Between the Revolution and de Gaulle's accession to power in 1958 there were seventeen different constitutions. Under the Fourth Republic alone (1946–1958), there were twenty-eight different governments, each averaging little more than five months in office. When a certain government fell the country did not come to a standstill; however, no *new* decisions could be made until another government was formed. Progress, in other words, was postponed. In practice, what often happens in the formation of the new government is that the man who was minister of agriculture becomes, say, minister of education. Portfolios are shifted on the political stage like the famous *guignol* puppets; a couple of controversial ministers are temporarily dropped from public office; and the new government takes over.

David Schoenbrun points out in his book *As France Goes* that the real source of the troubles in France does not lie only with the frequent changes of government; it lies in the continuous failure to modernize the economy and diplomacy, and this failure to modernize stems from many things: traditionalism in French life, skepticism on the part of the individual, and a conservatism that has existed since the great Revolution.

The French have so often been faced with the dilemma of whom to have confidence in that they have developed a contentiousness not only toward governments but toward any authority whatsoever. They are suspicious of their neighbors, whether they be the traditional enemy, the Germans, or the family living next door—not to mention the *Commissaire de Police* (police commissioner), the tax collector, or the local social security officer. This attitude has had serious effects on modern French life, where cooperation between governments, private industry, labor unions, and educational institutions is essential if progress is to be realized.

Structure of Government

General de Gaulle, the principal architect of the Fifth Republic, believed that the inherent ills of France could be solved only by a strong central government. He knew that real changes in France had taken place only when a strong leader was at the helm: Charlemagne, Louis XIV, Napoleon Bonaparte. De Gaulle had served a brief term as president in 1945 and retired in disgust when the people refused to accept the idea of strong executive government. De Gaulle was the kind of man who, if he was to rule at all, had to have the power to exercise his authority.

He drew up a new constitution which was approved in a referendum in 1958 and modified in 1962. The provisions were: The president of the republic was elected by direct suffrage for a six-year period by all citizens over twenty-one years of age; the president selected the premier and consulted with him in the choice of ministers—agriculture, interior, foreign affairs, education, transport, youth and sport, and so on; the president had the power to negotiate and to ratify treaties; he presided over the Council of Ministers; he could formulate laws, could dissolve parliament, and could call referenda (as de Gaulle did for Algerian independence in 1961 and 1962, and on other matters after that). In cases of emergency, the president could assume exceptional powers, which meant that he could rule, at least temporarily, by decree. Thus, the president of France became an executive with great power, and parliament was again in the position of serving him.

France's National Assembly is composed of 481 representatives (465 from metropolitan France, 10 from overseas *départements* such as Corsica, and six from overseas territories). The senators, of whom there are 273, are elected indirectly by an electoral college made up of deputies, general counselors, and delegates from municipal councils. Parliament votes on laws initiated by its members, the premier, or the president. In cases of differences between the two houses, reconciliation is tried. If that fails, the National Assembly law is adopted.

The sessions of the National Assembly, in which the government defends its policies, are often wild affairs. Cries and shouts, interruptions by opposition deputies, even occasional fistfights make up the scene. But this is democracy at work in France.

The job of the central government is to manage and defend the general interests of France. The country is divided into 95 *départements,* each of which is administered by a government-appointed *préfect* who has wide powers. The 38,000 cities and towns in the country are governed by elected mayors and councils. For example, in Chamonix, the mayor is the well-known mountaineer Maurice Herzog. There are twenty-three council members, and they meet from time to time to discuss issues of local importance. These meetings are open to all, and complete reports are published in *Le Dauphiné Libéré,* one of the important regional newspapers of France. When controversial questions arise, the council and the mayor may want to consult with the *préfecture* at Annecy, the capital of the Haute-Savoie *département,* of which Chamonix is a part.

In a metropolis like Paris, there are two *préfects* and two councils: the *Préfect* of the Seine, the *Préfect* of Police; the Municipal Council, and the General Council. The *Préfect* of the Seine is responsible for the management of all the municipal services, and the *Préfect* of Police is responsible for public order. The city is divided into twenty *arrondissements,* or sections, each of which has an appointed mayor. Other big cities like Bordeaux, Lyons, and Marseilles also have special arrangements, but only one mayor for the entire city.

In this structure there are numerous high government posts that can be awarded to loyal party members, who in turn have the power to appoint lesser officials—creating what we call "political plums."

The legal system in France is theoretically independent of the other branches of government and above politics. But promotion of judges to superior courts is a duty of the party in power. There are various courts, depending on the nature of the litigation. For example, the administrative courts deal with individuals who feel that the state or authorities have overstepped their bounds. The highest of these is the *Conseil d'État,* or Council of State, which resembles a supreme court. It was originally created to protect the state against individuals; in practice, it has developed in the opposite way: It tends to protect individuals from the vagaries of the state. In several cases, General de Gaulle ignored the Court's decision that the votes for certain

*The Place Vendôme in Paris.
The ground floors of the
buildings are faced with
arches. Pilasters stretch over
the next two floors, and the
roofs have dormer windows.*

referenda were unconstitutional. De Gaulle explained his actions by saying that he was the architect of the 1958 constitution and, therefore, he rather than the court was the best judge.

Charles de Gaulle for Good or Bad

For more than ten years, Charles de Gaulle ruled France. He was the strongest and longest-lasting executive since Louis Napoleon. De Gaulle's life and his political career are fascinating in any study, not only of France and the French but of world politics. When he died in 1970 at the age of seventy-nine, everyone admitted that *le grand Charles,* despite his faults and errors, was one of the towering political figures of the twentieth century.

From the first, de Gaulle was a man of history. If what he said was sometimes unpopular, he was at least a great actor, a fine speaker,

77

and a man who created emotion and excitement. He represented France like Vercingetorix, Louis XIV, and Napoleon. De Gaulle, known as the great traditionalist, ruled the country at a time when the economic and social life was changing with unprecedented rapidity.

Charles de Gaulle, though he preferred to be called *"mon Général,"* developed more as a politician than a soldier. He was born on November 22, 1890, at Lille. His father had aristocratic roots. In the thirteenth century a certain Richard de Gaulle was given the fief of Elbeuf by King Philip Augustus. De Gaulle's ancestors fought in the Battle of Agincourt and in various French wars. Besides being soldiers, many of these men had literary ambitions; and it is generally agreed that de Gaulle's *Memoirs,* and speeches, whether the content is agreeable or not, are examples of fine French writing.

De Gaulle had received a classical education at Jesuit colleges in France and Belgium. He was among the first ten in his class at the military officers' school of Saint-Cyr, fought in World War One, was wounded twice, and was taken prisoner by the Germans. After the war, he married the daughter of a Calais industrialist, taught military history at Saint-Cyr, then went to the war school for exceptional officers.

De Gaulle did not fit into the mold of typical post-World War One officers. Almost from the beginning he was swimming against the stream. This was clear in his book *Le Fil de l'Épée* (*Edge of the Sword*), published in 1931. In this work, de Gaulle was highly critical of the Maginot Line, which had been constructed after the war along the Rhine in order to protect France from invasion. In another book, *Vers l'Armée de Métier* (*Army of the Future*), published three years later, he predicted, in contradiction to what the old-line generals were saying, that in the event of another war, French troops could not be mobilized swiftly enough, that the new war would be unlike any which had preceded it. His book sold a few thousand copies and had no effect. Today, at St. Cyr, the pages of de Gaulle's books are read with admiration by young officers.

In 1940, after the French capitulated, a puppet government was set up in Vichy; de Gaulle, meanwhile, set up a Free French Movement in London. On the eighteenth of June, 1940, over BBC radio, de Gaulle gave his famous "Call to the French": "Has the last word been spoken? Must hope die now? Is defeat decisive? No! Nothing is lost for France!" Actually, few people in the country heard the broadcast, the first of many beamed from England during the bleak days of occupation.

When de Gaulle died, however, it was his 1940 "Call to the French" that was used to stimulate once again French hero worship. De Gaulle was heralded as the man who had saved the honor of France, and he was compared to Joan of Arc, among other great heroes.

In 1940, however, the French people had thrown up their hands because the general feeling was that the war had been lost and one had better make the best of a bad situation. The Vichy government was supported by conservative elements in the country, by the church, and by the French Academy. In London, de Gaulle insistently denied that the Vichy government had the legal right to speak in the name of France. Looking back to those times, there is something ridiculous, even pathetic, about the claims of de Gaulle. He was a suspicious character to the English, and even more to the Americans. Roosevelt and the State Department feared his dictatorial tendencies. For them, Vichy was the legitimate government. Consequently, during his years in London, de Gaulle was often given the cold shoulder, and for years afterward he was bitter over the fact that he was kept in the dark on many of the Allied plans. For him it was an insult that France should be treated as a second-class country, even if she had been easily defeated. Though his movement grew in numbers, de Gaulle never succeeded in establishing a true French government in exile during the war. However, many of the men who joined him then later became prominent figures in postwar governments.

"Crossing of the Desert"

In the first election after World War Two, the Communist party polled 5 million votes to 4.56 million for the Socialists and 4.77 million for the Catholic party, the Mouvement Républicain Populaire (M.R.P.). De Gaulle was elected president, but he had trouble forming a cabinet when the Communists demanded the top three ministerial posts—interior, foreign affairs, and national defense—which they felt they had a right to because of their majority vote. A compromise was arranged by the party chiefs: The defense department ministry was split in two, with the Communists holding down the new ministry of armaments. By January 1946, de Gaulle, thoroughly disgusted by political infighting, and feeling that the executive branch of government was too weak under the constitution then in effect, resigned. He had to wait twelve years for the political climate to change.

De Gaulle has described his life as having three periods: His "call to honor" was his wartime leadership outside of France; his "crossing of the desert" was his retirement in 1946; and his "salvation" was his years as president of the Republic.

In his "desert" period, de Gaulle was the spokesman for the French People's Rally party (R.P.F.). His speeches were demagogic, and people referred to him as the "French Führer." At that point in his career, his ideas were far to the political right—against labor unions, in favor of regaining French influence in Indo-China, and in favor of keeping Algeria as a French colony. Despite his conservative tendencies, he was distrusted by the rightists because he had allowed the Communists to have a seat in the government in 1945. De Gaulle, though, was still a visionary. By 1949, he warned against American influence in France. He believed, like Charlemagne, that France could lead the way, that the solution to Europe's problems lay in Europe, not through American leadership. In a moment of obvious despair in November 1953, he said: "Think by how many failures my life has been marked! First I tried to persuade the authorities to endow France with an armored force that would have spared us the invasion. Then after the disaster of 1940, I tried to persuade the government to go to North Africa. . . . Again I failed. I failed at Dakar. Then after victory I tried to maintain the unity I had formed around myself, but in vain. Later, in grave circumstances I again tried, but in vain. . . . If these failures had been mine, they would have been of no importance, but they were the failures of France."

De Gaulle succeeded in establishing an image, not only of a man of history with a destiny, but as the savior of his country, just as Joan of Arc became the savior of France at an earlier time. Here was this man, this political leader, rising above the rest, full of flowery phrases, fine speeches, and an unconquerable spirit. De Gaulle for the French became more than just a leader. As the years passed, he exhibited in his person all the fervor of a religious missionary on his first trip into the heathen wilds. He was like France itself: marvelous, inspiring, and insupportable.

The Algerian Putsch

The Algerian war was the stepping-stone for de Gaulle's rise to power. For a while it was a serious obstacle that stood in his way, but once he had settled the Algerian question he was able to rule practically as a dictator.

Algeria became a French protectorate in the 1830s, and was colonized by 1847. At first, the French attitude toward their African colonies—which, by 1919, came to include Tunisia, Morocco, Djibouti, Senegal, French Guinea, the Ivory Coast, Togo, French West Africa, French Equatorial Africa, Madagascar, and the Cameroons—was missionary in nature. The job of the French colonists was to spread French culture and know-how. Unlike Great Britain, metropolitan France could easily live without colonial resources. Thus, at first, economic exploitation was not uppermost in French policy. But the Franco-Prussian War turned French colonial indifference into imperialism. In Algeria, for example, even though the French Algerians, called *colons* (colonists), provided educational facilities, built hospitals, factories, railroads, and taught French in the schools, they considered the Algerians second-class citizens. "We've done so much for them" was the typical rationalization of the *colons* when they were interviewed or came to France on leave. The fact was that it was impossible for an Algerian who had been educated abroad to return home and obtain a responsible position. The economic and political life of the country was firmly controlled by the *colons,* many of whom had been born in Algeria. They, too, considered Algeria their home.

The independence of Morocco and Tunisia was recognized by the French in 1956, but Algeria was quite another problem. There was a strongly entrenched business community, and Algeria was the gateway to the rich oil fields in the Sahara desert. In November 1954, a nationalist reign of terror finally broke out, and by 1955 more than 170,000 French troops had been sent to Algeria to contain 15,000 rebels. Terrorism, counterterrorism, murder, and torture became the rule. On one side were the *colons,* protected by the French army; opposing them were the rebels. Among the French troops there was disease and discontent. The rebels controlled the mountains and terrorized the cities at night. Back in France, the cost of the war, or "police action," as it was called, was enormous. Then, terrorist bombings began to take place in France itself. Were the *colons,* a few of whom were extremely rich, worth civil war? French people began to wonder.

In 1958, several hundred thousand French *colons,* supported by the army, demonstrated in favor of French rule. Their slogan: *Algérie Française.* They took over government office buildings and set up a revolutionary committee. Without army support, Paris could do nothing; and there was fear that this revolt of the *colons* against the legal French government would result in a *coup d'état* in Paris as well. Already the revolt had spread to the island of Corsica.

In Paris there were the sounds of bombs exploding in certain *arrondissements.* Day and night there were identity checks on the streets, roundups of suspicious persons, searches and seizures of arms from automobiles and apartments. The atmosphere was tense and made even more so by the lack of a strong French leader. The Fourth Republic government seemed to be on the verge of losing control of the situation.

Salvation: The Return of de Gaulle

The army in Algeria was led by a group of officers of rightist tendencies—plus groups of professional soldiers from the Foreign Legion and the parachute battalions. Aside from these, the majority of troops were recruits, and it was extremely doubtful that they would take part in overthrowing the Paris government. Thus, the Algerian revolt leaders were stymied. They could not leave Algeria, because it would quickly fall into the hands of the rebels, and they could not effectively invade France. This dilemma, of course, became clear to the public much later; but de Gaulle was an old army man and knew what was going on.

Voting is an essential part of democracy in France. Every citizen over the age of twenty-one can vote, and there is a movement to extend voting rights to eighteen-year-olds.

French governments rose to power and fell with surprising rapidity. The country was running out of possible premiers. A financial crisis was averted through partial devaluation of the franc. In May, de Gaulle announced that he was ready to help if his country needed him. He was supported by his party, the Gaullists, who were in favor of a change in the constitution and the establishment of a new republic with a strong president. De Gaulle had little support from the conservatives, radicals, and socialists, but there was no one else, and the situation had become so bad that something extreme had to be done. Finally, there were the army rightists who had faith in de Gaulle simply because he was an army man. They counted on him to do nothing but protect the army and its interests.

On June 1, 1958, de Gaulle was accepted by the National Assembly as head of the government. One of his conditions was that for six months he be given decree powers, after which time a new constitution would be presented to the French people. Thus, de Gaulle was out of the "desert" and into his period of "salvation." Politically, he was still an untested quantity.

After de Gaulle became president, France was politically divided into one governing party, the Gaullists, and many smaller parties, most of which spent the next ten years fighting among themselves. The most unified of these parties were the Communists. They consistently voted against de Gaulle, mainly because he represented a strong force, and they knew that they would have no chance of gaining a foothold in the government, nor would serious economic and social reforms take place with the general as president.

The longer de Gaulle remained in office, the larger became his majority in the National Assembly. In the 1958 election, the Gaullists had 212 deputies; in 1962, 229; in 1967, 244; and in 1968 (*after* the May revolt and general strike!), 357 representatives in the Assembly.

Some historians have claimed that on the question of Algeria de Gaulle knew from the beginning that the colony was lost for France, that independence would have to be granted and French interests there sacrificed.

It is more likely that de Gaulle tried various solutions and gradually came to realize that there was no satisfactory compromise possible between the nationalist rebels and the *colons*. However, for some people who believed that Algeria would be "saved" for France by de Gaulle, the general has remained a traitor. They said: "He rose to power crying *Algérie Française* and then did an about-face."

By the end of 1960, it had become clear to the French Algerians that their role and power in Africa was coming to an end. Emigration to France was the only possible solution. On January 8, 1961, a referendum was held in France to see if the people favored de Gaulle's policies there. When the people voted *pour* (for) by almost a three-to-one margin, the French generals in Algeria, Challe, Jouhaud, Salan, and Zeller, revolted. Terrorism became widespread. The OAS, a terrorist organization, burned schools, hospitals, and farms rather than leave these to the Algerians; in metropolitan France there were frequent bombings by OAS sympathizers. By 1962, 750,000 French Algerians, generally referred to as *pieds noirs,* had emigrated to metropolitan France. The struggle for Algeria, which had dominated French life for five long years, was over. For the first time since the end of World War Two, France, under de Gaulle, had a stable government. Institutions could be built, policies followed to their logical conclusion, economic development take place.

But wars, particularly colonial struggles with civil-war overtones, leave deep scars. Algeria was a free country, and thousands of French families had lost their brothers, sons, lovers, and husbands. Armistice days and the Day of the Dead (November 2), when flowers were brought to the graveyards, took on new significance. The colonial struggles probably did more to turn young and old French people against future war than any other single factor. In some ways, de Gaulle realized this, but in other ways his policies were a failure.

De Gaulle generally was successful in reconciling, at least momentarily, French-German differences. He tried to strengthen France's international institutions. Aid to underdeveloped countries—usually those in the franc zone—increased. He worked for complete colonial disengagement, but tried to maintain French interests in the Sahara through cooperation with the Arabs, not domination. He believed in European confederation with a minimum of supranational control. For de Gaulle, France was still France and had to be independent to be great.

On the larger international scene, de Gaulle presented a fearsome figure. He was often pictured as anti-American, and many of his policies and attitudes seemed to substantiate that belief. Some people claimed that de Gaulle was anti-Jewish because he stopped sending French arms to Israel. During his tenure, however, several Jews were appointed ministers and members of his government. He withdrew French troops from NATO and vetoed the entrance of Great Britain into the Common Market. Great Britain did not want to join the Common Market,

General de Gaulle in his office in 1959.

but when the veto came, they were piqued that de Gaulle had said No. When he cried *"Vive le Québec libre!"* in 1967 in Montreal, most Canadians, and particularly government officials, were outraged at his dabbling in the domestic affairs of another country and giving open support to revolutionaries. Some French people passed off this insult as another example of the ravings of the old general, while others were stirred once more by a revival of a sense of nationalism.

It was in his final reform that de Gaulle failed most noticeably. He called for a return to the old-fashioned monetary system based on gold, a system long discredited by economists.

De Gaulle assumed power at a moment of near revolution, and ten years later left the republic in a state of domestic strife. Despite his vanity and arrogance, de Gaulle was a careful showman and a stickler for details. His press conferences were planned weeks in advance and were extremely formal. He memorized his speeches, and he was coached by an actor. His tall, gangling figure, his long nose, his pomposity provided excellent material to cartoonists and satirical writers. Next to him, Georges Pompidou was pale and lackluster. De Gaulle hated state banquets. He always was a quick eater, and his habits forced everyone else to hurry. On some occasions, half-empty plates were snatched from his guests. He never had raw fruit served at table, it took too long to eat. De Gaulle wanted to get on with other things, the issues of the day and of history. Eating for the general was a task, not the pleasure it is for most Frenchmen. Even as a private citizen, he lived relatively simply. On his death he was buried like a common soldier "without music or band or funeral call."

Education and the May 1968 Crisis

Stagnation is perhaps the only practical way of remaining faithful to one's principles.—ROBERT DE JOUVENEL

For many years, street demonstrations, whether they were concerned with education, social ills, or political problems, have been common in France. The field of education has been particularly unsettled. In university life there exists a formal gulf between student and professor, but both groups have often joined together and expressed opinions about the important questions of the day. Sometimes this takes the form of issuing statements to the press and audio-visual media; but more often, groups of students and teachers gather together, hold a meeting, and then march up and down the Paris streets shouting slogans and singing songs. Sometimes the police try to restrain them, and violence follows; more often, the demonstrations peter out and discussions continue in the cafés of the Latin Quarter, as the student section of Paris is called. This has been the traditional method France's intellectuals have used to bring their needs and opinions to the attention of the authorities.

By the 1960's, Paris was no longer the only city in France in which a student could get a good education. Universities had been opened or greatly improved at Bordeaux, Grenoble, Lille, Lyons, Nantes, Marseilles, Strasbourg, and in other cities as well. Moreover, the government had not only enlarged and decentralized the university system, but many new *lycées* (secondary schools for students between eleven and

Students going to classes at the Sorbonne. Political activity, as evidenced by the posters covering the pillars, has been intense since the 1968 student revolts, which led to a general strike and the promise of substantial reforms.

The Lycée Paul Valéry in Paris is one of France's more modern schools. A lycée *prepares teen-agers for their baccalaureate examination, which is usually taken between the ages of 17 and 19.*

eighteen) and primary schools had also been constructed. Were these facilities sufficient to absorb the postwar baby boom and the increased demands for higher education? And once students graduated, would they be able to find jobs that matched their training? These were two important questions facing the French early in 1968—a crucial year in French history.

The year started badly at the University of Nantes, an important industrial city on France's Atlantic coast. In February, the students in university housing projects demanded the right of free visits between male and female students. Demand rejected, they staged a one-day strike. This was but the beginning. In the months that followed, militant students picketed dormitories and the student restaurants. "Even at that time," said Marie Ligneau, a student of literature in the school of letters and science, "it took a lot of courage to say No to the strikers." Her friend, Jean Gravier, a student in the school of commerce, added:

90

"It was easier to remain silent than to try to break the picket lines. We needed curricular and housing reforms—there was no question about that—but many students, like myself, were against forced strikes. In the struggles that followed, real liberty of expression disappeared."

Why was the University of Nantes among the avant garde in the strikes that rocked the very foundations of France in 1968? What were the causes that brought French education to a point where all major universities and many *lycées* were closed and frequently occupied by students and, in some cases, by faculty members as well? Before trying to answer these questions, one must understand that in France the student, particularly the university student, has traditionally considered himself a part of a special social class. Until twenty or thirty years ago, very few working-class-family children were able to attend the universities, mainly because of the restraints of custom and financial problems. But since the end of World War Two, French universities have opened their doors wider, and the student has become more aware of

Marie-Annick Ligneau and Jean Gravier, two students at Nantes University, explain the conditions which led to the 1968 student uprisings in France.

the necessity for the education of the largest possible number of persons. The extension of the university system outside of Paris helped provide good facilities for more people.

The University of Nantes, in a city with shipbuilding yards, many factories, and an important aeronautics industry, had a student body with a larger proportion of working-class-family children than in certain other university towns. In the summer of 1967, the national government, in order to reduce soaring overhead costs, cut social security benefits, while the Nantes municipal authorities increased fares on the city's transportation system. The two financial pressures created major discontent among workers and their families at Nantes. In Paris the majority of students came from middle- or upper-class families (with the possible exception of the campus at Nanterre), and were less affected by financial pressures.

One demand of the more militant student strike leaders at Nantes was for more contact between the industrial life of the city and the university. As the strikes followed one after another and classes were held less and less frequently, strike committees not only demanded basic university reforms, but the right of workers, whether students or not, to eat in university restaurants. Even more important, they wanted workers to share in the direction of the university itself. This involved an important change, not only in the structure of the university but in society as well. Middle-of-the-road students, like Mlle. Ligneau, said that once the strike really got started in May, "one had the feeling that the students did not have their feet on the ground. They were carried away by their ideas." In that sense the educational revolt resembled the Revolution of 1789–1794.

Contacts with workers, M. Gravier indicated, were important. "We were not against their using the university restaurants if they wanted to; but in the direction of the university, difficult problems were posed, particularly since political points of view got mixed up with questions of pedagogy." By the end of May, two major questions had emerged: How should the university be reformed, and should one reform the society as well? For most of the students, who had limited time for university studies before they took jobs, the question of reforming all of society posed problems that they were not in a position to tackle.

While Nantes was in an uproar, unrest was also growing in Paris and other university towns. In April at Nanterre, where one of the new branches of the Paris university system had been established in a grim working-class district on the outskirts of the capital, militant students demanded the right to hold political meetings on campus and the right to smoke in class. They interrupted classes by slamming desk tops and screaming Marxist, Maoist, and anarchist slogans. They gradually gained support from calmer faculty members and students. They pointed up certain deficiencies, such as the fact that the school was half completed; public transportation to the "campus," if one could call it that, was practically nonexistent; and that there were no cafés,

The world-famous Sorbonne University, "La Sorbonne."

such as in the Paris Latin Quarter, where students could meet their friends and discuss all sorts of subjects.

With classes completely disrupted, university life could not continue. On May 3, Nanterre was closed by the rector. A rector, the head of one of the twenty-five regions called academies into which France is divided, is responsible to the ministry of education in Paris. Infuriated, many Nanterre students marched on the Sorbonne in Paris, whereupon the frightened rector called the police and gave them permission to clear and occupy the premises.

Since its founding in the thirteenth century, the Sorbonne had been an independent institution that had never been invaded by the forces of order. The physical presence of police inside the Sorbonne itself was an affront which did much to infuriate and unite many otherwise passive students. Fights and demonstrations began. Hundreds of persons on both sides were hurt; tear-gas fumes spread through Paris; explosions of Molotov cocktails rocked the city. Miraculously, no one was killed. Once again, the spirit of revolution was in the Paris air.

As the student revolt gained widespread support from many segments of the society, it was clear that the government had been caught off guard and had underestimated the importance of this sudden outbreak. Ten years of rule by de Gaulle had brought about complacency rather than wisdom. Foreign policy had been emphasized. Officials had been patting each other on the back because the economy had made some important strides forward; but now students and workers were claiming their part of the pie. Pompidou said later that during the Fifth Republic the budget for education had tripled and that hundreds of classrooms had been built. This was true enough and might impress television viewers. It could not, however, be stomached by students who had spent years in overcrowded amphitheaters, who had virtually no human contact with their professors who, in turn, were teaching under a system established by Napoleon.

On the fourteenth of May the workers at the Nantes Sud-Aviation plant occupied the premises and locked the directors in their offices. The same day, groups in Paris occupied the Odéon theater, setting off what they called the cultural revolution. Jean-Louis Barrault, the fa-

94

mous actor and director of Odéon, was on the side of the students. Later on in the year, after order had been restored, Barrault was fired. In addition, more than a hundred top journalists and reporters from the state-controlled radio and television networks were dismissed. During the crisis they had tried in vain to free French radio and TV from the controlling hand of the government.

Trade Unions and the Communist Party

What was the position of the trade unions? What was the reaction of the Communist party, the most cohesive and best-organized political group in France? Both organizations had been caught off guard by the magnitude of the student strike. They felt that the time for revolution had not yet come. The Communist party had been working for years to become "respectable" in order to enlist the support of large bourgeois segments of the population. Their attitude seems to have been that a general strike and drastic changes in society at that time would not succeed. The way would be opened either to anarchy or a military dictatorship. Furthermore, relations between the French government and the Soviet Union had been steadily improving. These long-range aims, they felt, were not to be destroyed by student unrest. The party was fighting for its life. Party members had not set off the revolt, and they disapproved of it. They distrusted the student leaders; their own authority was being threatened. Thus, they warned their followers all over France to keep their distance and prevent the students from entering factories and influencing the mass of workers. As Georges Séguy, the head of the Communist-led labor unions, said, "The workers don't need tutors."

Still, the situation reached a point where unions and Communists either had to support the movement or lose control over their adherents. With workers at Nantes, Cléon, and Flins already out, the labor unions gave the order for a general strike. At the same time, the order went out that there was to be no violence and no provocations. The restraint of the workers and their discipline during the difficult days of May probably did more than anything else to avert deaths and civil war.

On May 30, de Gaulle, having previously enlisted the support of army generals in the event of a real revolution, gave a firm speech: "Recreation period is over," he declared. He dissolved the National Assembly and called for new elections. Many people from all classes of life gave a sigh of relief. Once again there was someone in command of the rocky French ship of state. Suddenly one realized that many people had been genuinely afraid.

Three weeks of economic standstill and disorder had shaken the foundations of French society. People were saying that nothing in France would ever be the same again. But could that be true? Can a society which has evolved through the centuries be destroyed in a few weeks by a bloodless revolt? The French Revolution—a far more profound struggle—had only served to open the doors to a different form of reactionary government and the entrenchment of the bourgeois class. As Alfred Cobban wrote: "The tragedy of the French Revolution lay not in the reaping of a crop of dragon's teeth, but in the frustration of so many noble and apparently practicable aspirations. It was, in the words of Albert Schweitzer, a fall of snow on blossoming trees." The words can apply as well to the 1968 events. What, then, *had* the revolt of 1968 brought forth? In the end, workers got pay raises and fringe benefits, and the students, who had started the whole thing, got promises of eventual reforms.

Causes of the Educational Crisis

Many elements enter into the question of why French education—students, faculty, administration—revolted in May 1968. The postwar population explosion has been suggested, for it caused a shortage of teachers and crowded classrooms, difficult housing conditions for students and faculty members, and other problems; but this is not sufficient explanation for what is a complex problem.

In talks with students, professors, and education authorities, one name kept popping up: Napoleon. Professor Bonnet, who teaches history at Clermont-Ferrand University, pointed out that 160 years earlier Napoleon had said that he could look at his watch and tell what the students in the *lycées* were studying at that moment. The fact was that the French educational system in 1968, in its main lines, had changed little

96

Air France pilots Yves Ginocchio and Jacques Bourdet check the instruments of their medium-range Caravelle plane. After finishing the lycée *they studied a year at an engineering school and then five years at a civil aviation school.*

from the time of Napoleon, its founder. Napoleon's influence on French education was almost as important as his administrative code and its structure was terribly rigid.

Napoleon needed administrators and technical experts to serve the state. "In a properly organized state," he said, "there is always a body destined to regulate the principles of morality and politics." To provide such state servants, there developed three higher education schools— *les grandes écoles* as they are called—operated by the state to prepare state employees: the École Polytechnique—a military school which prepares engineers; the École Normale Supérieur—a teacher's college which prepares students for careers in the *lycées* and universities; and the École Nationale d'Administration, founded in 1945, which prepares civil servants. A diploma from any of these schools is the key to a high place in the French social structure. A graduate of the Polytechnique, for example, can aspire to be director of one of the nationalized industries; a graduate of the École Normale is a top intellectual, possibly even an important political thinker; a graduate of the École Nationale d'Administration may become a minister, a diplomat, or a member of the *Conseil d'État*. These schools, because of their extremely difficult entrance requirements, weed out all but the cream of the cream, and there is practically no lower-class representation. Sanche de Gramont points out: "What poses as a system for giving all candidates an equal chance is really a rationalization for the perpetuation of bourgeois elites."

Although the Constituent Assembly of 1791 gave every French citizen the right to be educated, it took about a hundred years to put that principle into practice. By 1820, more than half of the 38,000 towns in France had schools; but secondary education was not opened to women until 1880, and the rate of illiteracy was not significantly lowered until 1900. Although school is compulsory in France until the age of sixteen, until about 1955 the French *lycées* and universities received pupils mostly from the middle and upper classes. Moreover, French educational methods in primary and secondary schools were characterized by a system of awarding the smart children ribbons and medals, and failing to

After she had passed her "bac" (baccalaureate), nineteen-year-old Mlle. Binet decided that a university education did not offer enough security, and she decided to become a precision machinist at the Adult Training Center at Champs sur Marne.

98

recognize that in every student, whether bright or dull, there was some quality worth developing. The system of entrance and final examinations in many of France's higher education schools, and particularly in the three *grandes écoles,* came from the belief that competition was the best method of education.

Adult Education

About forty miles outside of Paris along the Marne River is a school that trains adults for periods ranging from one week to eleven months. One finds highly skilled persons like physicists who come to the center to learn new processes and techniques, and one finds persons who are learning a trade for the first time. The pupils spend an average of six hours in shops and an hour and a half in classrooms. In addition to their room and board, they are paid the national minimum wage, which comes to about sixty cents per hour, and, if they have had some previous training, they are paid about sixty dollars per month in addition while they are learning. Getting into this school is not easy. Of the four thousand applicants in 1969, only a thousand were selected.

Georges Bonnet was originally from Marseilles. After having worked for six months as a shoe salesman, he was drafted into the army. One day he attended a lecture dealing with the Adult Education School on the Marne River, and he was interested. He applied and passed the entrance examination three months later. He decided to specialize in electricity. After a year of training, he will take a job. The school regularly receives requests for qualified workers from branches of industry, and graduating students have little trouble finding work. Once on the job, M. Bonnet plans to continue his studies at night.

Another student at the school is Jean Crédoz, who was originally a bricklayer from the Haute-Savoie *département*. He decided to come to the school in order, as he said, "to climb the ladder a bit. If one stays where I was, you don't get very far. You just stay a worker all your life." Believing that he was capable of doing more than just laying bricks, he temporarily left his wife and child and came to Paris. He decided to study building methods and has been specializing in reinforced concrete. After ten months of study he will be able to work with engineers in the building trade. He too does not expect to have difficulty finding work.

Adult education is one of the better aspects of the French educational system. Many of the nationalized industries, such as the railroads, also operate apprentice schools and train young people for specialized tasks. In many cases, this training is not restricted to one field, but includes some general studies and foreign languages. In all of France, the National Railroad Schools have about three thousand apprentices in training. The teachers are persons who have worked for a period of time in the railroads and are recruited for short periods to train others.

Democracy and French Education

The most democratic and creative aspect of the French educational system are the *écoles maternelles,* or nursery schools. These state-supported schools, which accept children from two to five years of age, are nonobligatory and free. In 1970, more than 1.7 million French children attended them, and it is estimated that by 1975 the number will exceed 3 million. Created in 1881 for the children of the poor, they give children a chance to learn many skills: painting, modeling, singing, dancing, and so forth. They prepare the child for later schooling and give him the chance to adapt to a group milieu. They have the unique opportunity of ameliorating the social inequalities which are, unfortunately, still very much a part of life in France.

Inequality due to income or social status still has a profound effect on a student entering the regular school system. For a working parent, sending a child to school for so many years can be a burden. The government and certain industries are more and more turning their attention to this basic problem. The more they succeed, the fewer will be those French teen-agers who will be forced to go into professions and trades not of their choice.

Once the student is in the university, the cost of his education skyrockets. In France it is exceedingly difficult and against the concept of the intellectual to work one's way through school. Salaries are simply not high enough, and high-paying summer jobs are very rare. The student has to pay for his room and board, books, clothing, and so forth.

100

A French classroom.

So it is that the lower-class university student, particularly if he is living away from his home, is often in a precarious situation.

For this reason, universities are still predominately filled with students from the middle and upper classes. When they graduate, they have the best opportunities for posts in business, government, or in the professions. In this way, the class structure of French society is maintained from generation to generation. Only very slowly are class barriers breaking down so that all men and women can choose their future, not on the basis of their heritage, but on their individual talents and intelligence.

Despite its deficiencies, the standard of education in France is quite high. Teaching methods for the most part are traditional, and curricula are conservative. But graduates from the *lycées,* universities, and *grandes écoles* have a solid basis for further learning or for entrance into industry or the professions. Many pedagogues hope that during the 1970's leaders from government, education, industry, and labor will get together and fix firm and practical policies for education, and that French education can strive to be more democratic in its structure, more creative in its approach, and more fruitful in its results.

The Economic Situation

France is the only country in the world where if you add ten citizens to ten others you do not make an addition but twenty divisions.—PIERRE DANINOS

Napoleon Bonaparte admitted that in his attempts to conquer foreign lands, 1.7 million Frenchmen died. In World War One, France lost 1.4 million men, and 4 million more were wounded. In World War Two another 800,000 men were killed, and out of the 2 million taken prisoner, more than 200,000 died in Germany.

In addition to war losses, at the beginning of the nineteenth century the population of France decreased because the fertility rate went down. More people died than were born. Finally, until the 1950's, there was very little immigration into France. Early in the nineteenth century the population of France represented one seventh that of Europe; in 1970, France's population represented one fifteenth. From 1870 until World War Two, the population of France did not grow, despite the anti-birth-control laws of the 1920's and special benefits granted to parents who produced large families. With a population of forty million, France remained basically a rural country with many small towns, several medium-sized cities, and one huge metropolis—Paris—where one seventh of the French people lived.

Late in the 1960's, birth control laws were altered. Now, French women can buy contraceptive pills in drugstores with a prescription, and contraceptive devices can legally be prescribed by doctors. Family planning centers also became legal.

A small boy plays with a water fountain on the old cobblestoned streets of Cognac.

Aside from all the suffering and misery they brought, the wars left France with a population of very old and very young citizens; in France today just under 40 percent of the population of 50 million is "active"; that is, supports the other 60 percent, which includes some women, students, small children, the old, the infirm, and the unemployed.

The Troubled Farmer

These population factors have had a strange effect on agriculture. Jean-François Breton, the director of the 800,000-member Federation of French Agricultural Unions, pointed out that according to the census of 1955 (the latest complete one available), the average age of the 1.4 million French farmers was fifty-six years. The reason for this, he said, could be traced to the fact that many young to middle-aged farmers were killed in the First World War. Their infant sons were left to inherit the land and are now in their fifties. Of the farmers who were interviewed in the census, 96.7 percent had had no more education than their fathers. Brought up during the war, much of the rural population had little opportunity to go to school. If a farm boy was lucky, he received a primary school certificate at the age of fourteen.

This lack of education has retarded the modernizing of French farms. "In certain rural villages," M. Breton said, "we find farmers who use the same methods that were used by their fathers and grandfathers, and a few farmers who use modern methods." Even though France is third in world production of milk and butter, second in wine and cheese, and fourth in meat, hand milking, the use of horse and plow for tilling and cultivating, and old-fashioned cattle-production methods are still widespread. The increased number of tractors on French farms is impressive, but many farmers do not know how to get the most efficient use out of them. The education of farmers in the use of modern machines is a major task of the French farmer's union. But, as M. Breton pointed out, before one can teach new methods one has to convince old farmers of their validity. This is being done through farm publications and frequent visits by union representatives.

As is true in all developed countries, the French farm population is diminishing. Farmers and their children migrate to the cities, where

On most French farms the tractor has taken the place of the horse-driven plow. However, some small farmers, like Charles François, here seen plowing grape vines, still use old methods.

there are opportunities for schooling and jobs in industry. But important efforts are being made to help the farmer adapt to the modern world. This is particularly necessary because France is the largest agricultural country among the six members of the Common Market. Revenues from exports of farm produce help to make possible the purchase of crude oil, of which France has little, and of certain metals that are in short supply among the six. Incidentally, one probable reason why General de Gaulle vetoed the entry of Great Britain into the Common Market was because he was aware that if Great Britain were admitted, serious, possibly devastating, changes would have to be made in the French agricultural price structure. At that time, many

British people were against Common Market membership because, at least initially, it meant a rise in consumer food prices.

But as M. Breton knows so well, traditional methods of farming are difficult to change. "The influence of the old farmer on French agriculture is enormous," he said. "Change takes time, and farmers' unions are trying to speed up the process." One of the ways the unions are doing this is to spread the idea that farmers, like other workers, must retire at a certain age. Thus their land inevitably becomes the property of younger, more progressive-minded farmers. Another problem of the French farm is its size. The average farm consists of only 12.8 acres. In some cases, the farms are too small to provide a decent livelihood. With union encouragement, a movement has begun to amalgamate three to five small farms into corporations that can share production methods and profits. There are many thousands of these farm corporations in France, and their number is increasing.

In addition, there is the Society for Arranging Farms (SAFER), an association that buys small farms, groups them into larger units, and redistributes them. As more and more of France's old farmers sell out, retire, or die, French farms will tend to become larger and more efficient.

Other methods are being used to strike at the heart of traditional farming procedures. Through the auspices of the *Centre d'Étude Technique Agricole* (Technical Agricultural Study Bureau), ten to twenty farmers who are not in competition with one another get together and hire an agricultural expert. This person, partially paid by the government, helps these farmers to choose machines and animal feeds, and even aids in farming accounting procedures.

A Progressive Farmer

Guy Estanove is a farmer from the hamlet of Mas Grenier in southern France, not very far from the city of Toulouse. The Tarn-et-Garonne region, where he lives with his wife and six children, produces grains such as alfalfa, corn, and wheat. Until the year 1965, M. Estanove's principal crop was alfalfa, which was well suited to the region. Through the Paris grain market, he sold the alfalfa for export to Scandinavia and West Germany. In 1965, however, the bottom fell

When farmer Guy Estanove had difficulty making a living, he turned part of his land into a small zoo.

out of the market. Italy and Yugoslavia were also producing alfalfa; there was a large overproduction, and the price fell by about fifty percent.

At that price, M. Estanove calculated, it did not pay him to plant alfalfa, and so he looked around for some other crop to plant, or some other business to enter in order to make a living from his 144-acre farm. Other farmers had planted fruit trees. Some considered tobacco, but that involved important capital investment, not to mention know-how which few in the region had. While looking for a solution to his problem M. Estanove continued planting alfalfa in the hope that the price would go up to at least forty cents a pound, either by an increase in the demand or through government subsidies. It didn't. By 1969, farmers who had quickly switched from alfalfa to fruit farming were also losing money: There was an overproduction of fruit, and export markets were dominated by the Italian fruit growers.

107

It occurred to the Estanoves that their farm, because it bordered on the Garonne River, one of the principal inland waterways of France, rising in the Pyrenees and flowing all the way to Bordeaux, was an ideal site to build a small hotel and swimming pool. M. Estanove drew up plans describing this project, and since he also liked small animals, he included the possibility of eventually constructing a small zoo. He approached local and *département* authorities. "Lots of people talked with big ideas, but when I got around to asking about loans and authorizations for this sort of thing, no one knew anything."

Finally, one bank offered him a low-cost loan. The sum offered was not sufficient to construct a hotel and swimming pool, but was enough to build a zoo. So M. Estanove, despite the fact that his neighbors thought him crazy, began building cages and importing animals.

"Go on planting your alfalfa," he told them "just like your fathers and grandfathers. At twenty-five cents a pound you'll soon all be bankrupt."

Through newspaper and television advertisements, and a lot of talking around, M. Estanove's zoo, containing monkeys, anteaters, birds of many different sorts, foxes, deer, and serpents, became known. On a few Sundays during 1969 when the weather happened to be fine, more than a thousand visitors were registered. At an admission price of three francs (about sixty cents), M. Estanove made close to six hundred dollars per Sunday. His neighbors began to wonder.

Year around, of course, the going was hard, but at least M. and Mme. Estanove had the courage to start a new business. They hope that eventually they will be able to build the tourist hotel and swimming pool.

Understandably, M. Estanove is very pessimistic about the plight of the French farmer. Taxes on his land and on what he buys, as well as social security dues for his family and one hired hand, have increased tremendously. "The economy is under absolutely no firm national controls. One year there is a shortage of potatoes, and the next year every one plants them, so there is an overproduction. And the same thing happens with eggs, melons, and grain. If you ask the *département* agricultural authorities what to plant in order to make ends meet, they

108

are incapable of telling you. And whenever the government establishes a policy for the farmers you can be sure it will not work."

In France, complaining is as much a French specialty as wine with the cheese. What is of importance in what this farmer has to say is that in France there is a lack of intelligent, careful, long-range planning with price controls and possibly with subsidies as well. In his view the French farmer has tended to bear the brunt of unstable government and its confused agricultural policy.

Cattle Raising

If you were to visit the 240-acre cattle farm of Hubert and Jacques Bezard-Falgas, not far from M. Estanove's property, you might think you had suddenly been transported to Texas. There are large fields with fences around them, a long cattle shed where hundreds of beef cattle are carefully tended, bred, and fed. The machinery is modern. The farm grounds are spick-and-span. Only the main farmhouse, built of stone some two hundred years ago, might make you doubt that you were in the American West.

In 1951, Hubert spent a year in the United States, where he learned a great deal about cattle farming. He also visisted model farms in Scandinavia and Germany. Meanwhile, Jacques studied business and accounting. When Hubert and his brother inherited their father's land, they decided to set up a cattle farm on a scientific basis, making use of their joint knowledge.

For the past fifteen years they have developed the reputation of being avant-garde cattle producers. They receive visitors from all over Europe, and they now have to turn them away. "If we didn't do that," said Hubert, "we wouldn't get any work done at all." Still, despite the interest in their work, they are discouraged. They feel that after all their efforts they should be registering important profits instead of barely breaking even. The cattle business is so uncertain that Hubert has discouraged his sons from taking over the farm when they finish their university schooling. Many of the reasons the brothers give for their lack of success are similar to M. Estanove's and could apply to farmers

Hubert and Jacques Bezard-Falgas raise steer scientifically on their model 240-acre farm southwest of Toulouse.

all over the world: The price of production is too high in proportion to what they get back in profits. The reason is that state and social security taxes are too heavy. Hubert says with bitterness, "We are badly governed in France." He believes that the French, like many other Latin peoples, are extremely difficult to govern. "French people," he says, "just don't see the value of organizing."

His brother Jacques explained their lack of success in economic terms: Prices of calves have gone up, while the price for fattened beef has remained pretty much the same. A special problem for the French cattle producer is the large number of wholesalers between the producer and the consumer. "Sometimes," Jacques said, "there are as many as five intermediaries, each of whom gets his share and reduces our profits."

To combat this problem, several producers of cattle have joined forces

110

and are attempting to sell directly to butchers, either in France or through the Common Market. "Still, we are incapable of establishing any real long-range planning mainly because of the lack of organization of the French in the Common Market. We don't know what price our cattle will get . . . while we are held to the price of lean calves." When asked about the possibility of establishing cooperatives to handle all aspects of meat production and sale, both brothers felt that although this was successful in Scandinavia and certain other countries, it could not work in France "because the people just aren't disciplined enough."

The government is very much aware of many of these problems and is working hard to remedy them. Through grants, more extensive planning, and a demand that the public accept the financial burdens reforms will involve, they hope to bring French farming, so important to the economy of the country, up to a par with farming methods in other highly developed countries.

The Industrial Revolution

As we have seen, although the French Revolution and succeeding ones as well in 1830, 1848, and 1870, gave vent to certain liberal ideas, in effect postrevolutionary France became more conservative than before. During the nineteenth century, when exciting reforms of the social structure and of industry were taking place in other European countries, conservatism deepened among France's controlling powers. One important aim of the Bank of France, where wealth was centered, was to guard against any social or economic change. The same was true for industry, where experiment or change was discouraged. "A rigid protectionism," writes Alfred Cobban, "shielded French industry from competition and the compulsion of progress." The propertied classes in whom power was centered were also dominated by the idea of no change: "Live as the bourgeois, and live nobly" was their aim. The church supported these classes and issued "spiritual sanctions against those who would attack" them.

High civil servants in government administration were the sons of the rich, interested only in keeping their jobs and serving any master that provided security. Idealism had little place in practical French life. The influence of French thinkers and philosophers was stronger outside of France than within.

Thus, while other countries were developing and changing rapidly, until 1880 France remained practically stagnant. Some changes, of course, could not be avoided. Between 1820 and 1850 a few blast furnaces were introduced, as well as mechanical weaving machines. From 1850 to 1895 an extensive railroad network and an inland canal system were built. This stimulated the coal and steel industries. From 1855 to 1867, France's foreign commerce increased threefold. By 1910 France had become the world's greatest producer of luxury goods—fine fabrics, perfumes, cosmetics, gloves, pocketbooks, and *objets d'art* of all kinds. Throughout the world France became better known for its frivolities than for its industrial strength. In the public mind, fine wines, champagne, cognac, fashion, cheeses, and perfumes were synonymous with France.

The real development of industrial France did not get under way until the beginning of the twentieth century. Then dams were constructed for electric power, textile and chemical industries grew in the north and around the city of Lyons, armaments and gunpowder industries were installed to the west and southwest of Paris, and after World War Two the aircraft and nitrogen industries grew up in southwest France. To the east, around the provincial capital of Strasbourg, the coal and steel industries burgeoned. But by the late 1950's, the coal mines became less important, and many industries in the Nord and Pas-de-Calais *départements* had difficulty converting to new products. Conversion was necessary because the emphasis in France had shifted from complete protectionism to meeting competition of other Common Market countries. As industries grew and became more mechanized, they absorbed, through mergers or competition, the small workshops: independent furniture makers and cabinetmakers, shoemakers, metalworkers, and suppliers of the luxury-goods trade. These people either went out of business, took employment in larger companies, or had a very hard time making ends meet.

Today, France is among the world's top ten in production of iron ore, nickel, sulfur, bauxite, coal, steel, electricity, and cement. France is known for its production of automobiles, tires, and gasoline, and for cotton and wool yarns, and synthetic textiles. New industries, particularly in the electronics field, are taking on greater importance. French research workers and scientists are often among the best in their field. Charles Aplin, an American physicist from the University of California, who has been working in the research department of the Compagnie Générale d'Électricité, twenty-five miles outside of Paris, said, "French engineering may be the very best in the world." One concern of French industry is to try to keep this talent in the country. The only way they can do that is to offer salaries and opportunities as good as these qualified men and women can get abroad. At the moment, that is a hard task, because French wage scales, even for highly skilled persons, are much lower than in many other developed countries.

François Nicolas, a 29-year-old electrician from Saint Malo, uses a bicycle to get around the huge turbine room of the Rance Tidewater Dam.

As late as the 1950's, the country had a huge number of small businessmen and shopkeepers. Indeed, in 1954 there were more self-employed persons in business than employed in industry.

A citizen from Narbonne, who is a militant member of the French Communist party, conjectured that the 1968 defeat of de Gaulle was due, not to the Communists, union organizers, extreme leftists, or rightists, but to the increased organization of the businessmen of France. "The commercial elements in the country were fed up with the taxes and problems which came into effect during the past few years. The Communist party had been against de Gaulle since 1945, but when these small shopkeepers also finally turned against him, that was his downfall —and a great stride forward."

Many of France's shopkeepers are now organized into a union that calls itself the Small and Medium-Sized Enterprises (PME). This businessman's union, which is formed of shop owners and manufacturers who employ five to five hundred workers, claims to represent about 60 percent of the French productive capacity. The PME has a double function: to defend the interests of their members in conferences with the government, and to aid businessmen who want to modernize their factories. Early in 1968, the PME twice organized one-day strikes. As shop doors closed, cities, towns, and villages throughout France suddenly grew quiet. PME members protested "extraordinary abuses"—proportionately higher taxes for small business concerns than for large enterprises, for instance. Small businessmen were also fed up with a tax called the added-value tax (TVA) which they claimed was so complicated to calculate that a public accountant had to be engaged.

When it comes to complaining, French businessmen are probably as apt as the farmers. Still, the basic problem remained: What was the function of the small businessman in France? Should the government, through taxes and other pressures, force small businessmen to modernize, expand, or go out of business? "Since the strikes, which were 90 percent effective, and the change in presidents," said a representative of the PME in an interview, "we believe that the government will come to terms with us. If not, there will be more strikes. One thing is

114

Dominique Tulasne, general secretary of the Young Business Directors Association, explains the problems facing French businessmen.

clear: Since the strikes, the small and medium-sized enterprises in France are more united than ever before."

The problem of bringing a nation of shopkeepers and small factory owners into more modern ways will be one of the painful and politically delicate tasks of the government in the future.

Young Executives

M. Dominique Tulasne is the general secretary of an organization called the Young Business Directors, which has about three thousand members none more than forty-five years old, who are heads of French companies. Meeting for seminars from time to time, this group aims to stimulate the development of French industry by reorganizing workers in a more efficient manner, thereby increasing production. M. Tulasne explained that certain traditional attitudes toward business are still very much alive in modern France. For example, for centuries, the family has played a dominant role in the structure of French industry; and this fact often prevented expansion and efficiency. "In France," he said, "if you sell your business, even for a profit, this is a sign of failure. Some businessmen prefer to go bankrupt rather than sell when there is still time to break even. The *esprit* of the French businessman is similar

115

to that of the peasant: one does not sell the land. Property is sacred, and to sell it is a crime."

M. Tulasne indicated that until 1964 it was impossible for a businessman to borrow money for longer than a seven-year period. And even if he wanted to make capital improvements in his business, it was exceedingly difficult to obtain creditors. The laws, however, have been changed, and now it is possible to borrow money and have up to twenty years to pay it back.

Another hangover from time immemorial is the idea of the *patron*. "In France, the *patron* is the person who makes the decisions." M. Tulasne pointed out that in modern business, decisions have to be the result of group action: The heads of all branches of a company get together and decide as a group what is in the best interests of the company. In France, tradition had dictated that the *patron,* right or wrong, knowing or unknowing, was the boss; and this business dictatorship is one of the practices the Young Business Directors group is trying to change.

Gold and Taxes

Another traditional practice of French businessmen has been to convert business profits into gold, or invest them in firms in foreign countries. For centuries French businessmen, large or small, had little confidence in the stability of the franc. Consequently, private hoarding of gold prevented needed capital improvements from taking place, and many factories even today use the same methods and machines that were installed in the 1920's.

For the businessman gold had a fixed value, but the franc—who knew what would happen? There have been many devaluations of French money. Money put into the bank at high interest rates had often been withdrawn ten years later worth half its original buying power.

Besides stability, gold had another advantage. It had always been difficult to collect taxes in France, and gold coins in the mattress or cupboard were hard to trace. Realizing that the Frenchman was by tradition a tax evader, the government established a system of low taxes on personal incomes. At the same time, heavy direct and indirect taxes took up the slack. Through the TVA, everything bought in France is taxed. This includes bread, milk, wine, perfume, automobiles, and so forth. The head of the Bordeaux Winegrower's Association bitterly complained to me about the fact that wine was taxed at 14 percent—close to the luxury-item rate—instead of being considered an agricultural product, which would reduce the tax to 6 percent. The lower tax, he felt, would make the good-quality Bordeaux wines more competitive domestically.

Unlike graduated taxes, which increase in proportion with higher incomes, everyone in France—rich or poor—pays the TVA. Many people feel that this form of taxation not only is unjust but has kept French prices higher than in other Common Market countries. A journalist recently calculated that, all things considered, the Frenchman pays proportionately as much tax as his American counterpart. Still, although the government may have devised a sure way to fill the state coffers, many businessmen either invested their money abroad or added to their private stock of gold.

Nationalized Industries and Private Unions

In 1927, the French airlines were nationalized; in 1928 the government took over the broadcasting network; in 1933, government took control of transatlantic shipping; in 1936, of railroads and armaments. After World War Two government control was extended to gas and electricity, the four largest banks, thirty-four insurance companies, the coal mines, called the *Charbonnages de France,* which also produced textiles and synthetics, the Renault automobile factories, and the Havas advertising company. Owning in all more than four hundred companies, the government is the largest employer in the country; and though it is little known, there are more nationalized industries in France than in Sweden.

A good many of France's nationalized industries are run not so much to make profit as to satisfy political and social goals. High administrative posts are excellent political plums for loyal party workers. Whom you know is often more important than what you can do.

Young workers on the assembly line of the Renault automobile works.

Featherbedding—use of two or three men to handle a one-man job—has traditionally kept unemployment rates down; and in the case of the French National Railways has resulted in consistent financial losses.

The French labor unions, which grew out of the socialist movements before the turn of the century, are in favor of nationalized industries, and any attempt to change this setup is met by firm resistance. Labor unions became legal in 1884, but did not win the right to recruit members, hold meetings, and collect dues on company time until the 1968 general strikes; and they fight tooth and nail against any reduction in the labor force. The principal unions are the Communist-dominated *Confédération Générale des Travailleurs* (CGT), the largest; the more than one-million-member *Force Ouvrière* (FO); and the *Confédération*

Française Democratique du Travail (CFDT). The unions have had an unusually hard time organizing workers in such a conservative, tradition-ridden country as France. Strikes were often broken, sometimes even by conscripting workers, as Aristide Briand did in 1910, into the army. In some cases, unions simply did not have sufficient finances to withstand long strikes. Thus, one-day or one-week work stoppages became the usual form of protest. In addition, the unions are divided along ideological lines, some believing in violent overthrow of the government, some in nationalization of more industries, some in closer cooperation with the *patrons,* and so forth. Each union tends to side with a particular political party and, at election time, directs its members to vote for that party's candidates.

The French labor movement is divided by many forces but most of all by its inability to act together for common goals. For example, in 1969 the CGT called for a half-day work stoppage at the Renault auto plant at Boulogne-Billancourt. The CFDT reluctantly complied in order to maintain "union solidarity"; but André Bergeron, the progressive general-secretary of the FO, did not see the utility of such a short work stoppage. He wanted an unlimited strike. The FO workers stayed on the job. Thus, only part of the workers in the Renault plant went out on strike—for half a day. What was achieved by this is questionable.

Despite diversity and lack of finances, French trade unions have become a part of the industrial scene. It is likely that their influence will continue to grow. To the old aims of higher salaries, more leisure time through shorter work weeks, and security and dignity for the worker, unions have added three new demands: more responsibility for workers, a larger role in the management of firms, and a tie-in between the rising cost of living and real buying power.

Immobility of the French

Until the 1960's, one of the characteristics of the French labor force was the workers' reluctance to leave the region in which they were born for work in another part of the country. "Engineers in France do not like to change from one job to another," said Albert Peres at France's Compagnie Générale d'Électricité. M. Peres is thirty years old and responsible for a group of thirteen persons who work on developing electronics products for industry. "They have a different way of looking at things. Lodging is hard to find, and once established they do not want to change their life. When a French person considers changing his work, he quickly sees that there is not much difference between working in Paris or Lyons. So why not stay at home?" This point of view is true for unskilled as well as skilled labor. The most extreme regional nationalism can be found in Brittany. Even though this region is one of the poorest in France, many of the inhabitants are so attached to the life and traditions there that even higher-paying jobs a hundred or two hundred miles away cannot tempt them. If they do migrate to Paris or Strasbourg, it is often on a temporary basis.

Recent statistics show, however, that the traditional immobility of

Fishmongers on the Brittany coast sell the day's catch to housewives. Note the tall white "coif and the wooden shoes worn by the woman.

Annot is a picturesque summer resort in the French Alps that is a favorite spot for the residents of Nice.

the French is slowly changing. Between 1962 and 1968, for example, one out of every fifteen Frenchmen changed regions. The Paris region, of course, was the most important center of attraction; but more than 600,000 Parisians, particularly older people, left Paris for the Midi—Provence, Côte d'Azur, Aquitaine. The northern part of the country —Lorraine, l'Auvergne, Basse Normandie, and Poitou regions—sent more of their citizens to Paris than they received in return. Migration between regions was also brisk. Inhabitants of the Lorraine went to Alsace, and the central part of France received many migrants from the Loire, Bretagne, and other regions. Only seven out of twenty-one regions increased in population of French, but during the same period a half million foreigners, mostly from Portugal, Spain, and Italy, immigrated to France. Many of these men and women were unskilled laborers who were attracted by higher salaries and steady work. In many cases, they were taking the place of French persons who no longer wanted to do manual labor. Many foreign laborers were lured into France by unscrupulous contractors who paid them the minimum hourly wage fixed by the government; and on this wage it was practically impossible to live. These workers' only protection against exploitation came from labor unions, which were not always successful in their arguments with the French *patrons*. With so many people moving around France, whatever regional traditions remain are disappearing very rapidly.

Le Défi Américain

At a time of social unrest in 1967, Jean-Jacques Servan-Schreiber, the French journalist who has since become general secretary of the Radical party and a member of the National Assembly, published his book *The American Challenge (Le Défi Américain)*. This book, originally intended for a limited audience of French businessmen, in six months' time sold more than half a million copies. And when the book was translated it became a best seller in many foreign countries as well. Its popularity might be ascribed to the fact that it attacks French business traditions and the established order. The main thesis of Servan-Schreiber's book is that after the war, American industry—all-knowing and powerful—jumped into the breach and took over old firms or established new industries on the Continent. This had become so flagrant that the entire structure, not only of European business society but of its political life, was threatened. Economic control of a country's business—American investments in Europe probably exceed $14 billion—is a form of colonialism. Servan-Schreiber warned that if Europeans did not soon wake up, Americans back in Dallas and Detroit would soon be in complete control of one of the world's most highly developed industrial areas. "We [Europeans] are witnessing the prelude to our historical bankruptcy," he wrote. "The invasion of the Americans into postwar Europe was the first full-scale war to be fought without arms or armor."

122

Servan-Schreiber believes that only through an economically united Europe, including in the Common Market the Scandinavian countries, Great Britain, and possibly Spain as well, can Europeans hope to meet the American challenge. Modern business schools are needed to teach management and marketing techniques, and a radical change in thinking has to be made by the French and European businessmen. The real shock came in Servan-Schreiber's clear exposé of how France has become the victim of a new kind of war—an economic one. It was disquieting that the old land of Gaul had been so discreetly invaded; the problem was that no one had any quick solutions. Nationalist cries of "Save French industries for the French" were met by comments such as,

Workers picking flowers in Grasse, a leading center of French perfume industry near Nice. Besides perfumes, Grasse is also known for its fruit preserves and its crystallized flowers.

Monday is washday all over the world. A few French women still wash their clothes in village fountains or streams, but by far the majority prefer electric washing machines.

"If we don't accept the American industrialists, some other Common Market country will."

There have been critics of Servan-Schreiber's thesis. The American journalist John Hess, in his book defending de Gaulle, writes: "With six members, the market has enormous difficulty in reaching decisions on relatively minor issues and in making its decisions stick. . . . What in the world makes Servan-Schreiber think it would be easier to reach such decisions with eleven members?" Hess suggests that rather than compete with the American giant, perhaps France and other European countries would be better off specializing in a few industries. He points

124

to the successful competition of Japan and Sweden. In any case, particularly now that de Gaulle is dead, it seems unlikely that France will force American business interests out of the country. After all, French and American interests are closely entwined.

Many persons have been critical of the fact that precious years have passed without basic renovations taking place in French agriculture, industry, housing, education, and social institutions. During the early 1960's, sufficient government leadership and money just were not available. Without those two elements the inherent French resistance toward change could never be overcome.

France, however, still led the world in luxury goods like perfume, wine, and fashion design. By the late 1960's it became clear that basic changes were going on in the national economy and the outlook of businessmen. Government, labor, and industry leaders were under severe pressure to institute meaningful reforms. This pressure came from inside, and from outside the country as well. It was evident to all that once the wealth of France's natural resources and know-how are more efficiently exploited, the standard of living of her people will rise dramatically. The people want it; progress can no longer be postponed.

Invention and Creation

In France, the first day is for tasting, the second for criticism, and the third for indifference.—J. F. DE LA HARPE

In 1971 it was announced that France, together with West Germany, Switzerland, Italy, Belgium, and Austria, intends to build a 300-billion-electron-volt atom smasher. When completed in 1978, this will be the largest accelerator in the world. It is the most ambitious project ever undertaken by the European Organization for Nuclear Research (CERN), of which France is a member. Of particular note was the fact that, at a time when its economy was in difficulty, France had agreed to pay 30 percent of the $350 million costs.

Also in 1971, the French-British supersonic plane, the Concorde, was flown to South America. Though criticism from ecologists and doubts about its economic viability and practicality have been strong, for the French this has always been a prestige project. They went ahead in order to be among the first world manufacturers of supersonic transport planes. Thus, the Concorde's purpose was not just to carry passengers more rapidly during the 1970's, but to boost the national morale.

Other ambitious projects, such as the turbotrain, which, once the tunnel under the English Channel is built, will link the center of Paris to the center of London in three hours' time, is on the drawing boards and being debated.

Strictly national manufacture is becoming a thing of the past. Com-

The misty silhouette of the Eiffel Tower looms up behind these boys enjoying an afternoon of roller skating.

Although the construction of the multimillion-dollar Concorde *was hotly contested in France and Great Britain, it was built and test-flown in 1969.*

ponent parts for the above-mentioned inventions are manufactured in many parts of the world, and the studies which made them possible may have taken place in Japan or in Great Britain. In some cases, parts are shipped into France and assembled; in other cases, they are manufactured in France under license. France and most other European countries do not have complete technical facilities for manufacturing and assembling the complicated equipment that will be in use during the next decade.

The Inventive Spirit

The atom smasher, the Concorde, and the turbotrain are but a few of many highly ambitious projects that French researchers, engineers, and technicians are working on at the present time. They are the products of a long tradition of experimentation motivated by the desire of the French to learn more about the world and themselves. In the past, as at present, great inventors and scientists have been complemented by highly trained technicians and civil servants. They have often pushed ahead despite the machinations of politicians and private interest groups.

Examples of the French inventive spirit abound in France's history. Napoleon Bonaparte offered a prize of twelve thousand francs to the person who discovered a method of preserving food. The prize was won by an obscure inventor, François Appert (1750–1841), who is generally considered to be the father of the canning industry. Canned foods were one of the things that made Napoleon's far-flung war campaigns possible.

A blind man, Louis Braille (1809–1852), developed a system of raised dots placed in different combinations on stiff paper. Through these symbols blind people could read with their fingers. Although many new devices for the blind have been developed, Braille writing is still one of their important tools for normal living. Dr. René Laënnec (1781–1826) developed and popularized the stethoscope. The physicist and mathematician André Ampère (1775–1836) invented the electromagnet, which led to the electromagnetic telegraph. He also made important contributions to the fields of mathematics, chemistry, and philosophy. In the early 1800's Nicéphore Niepce (1765-1833) dis-

This blind man from Carcassonne is able to lead a fuller life because of the discoveries of Louis Braille.

129

covered photography, which was followed by the daguerreotype by Louis Jacques Daguerre (1789–1851), and by cinematography pioneered by Louis Lumière (1864–1948). Neon and fluorescent lights were developed by Georges Claude (1870–1960). Frenchmen invented the adding machine, the airship, the balloon, the gyroscope, smokeless powder, phosphorous matches, the machine gun, and the thermometer, and they have led the world in designing ships and racing craft. Important discoveries in the atomic sciences and of radium were made by Pierre and Marie Curie, for which they won the Nobel Prize in 1903 and 1911. The list of French inventors and their discoveries goes on and on.

The Legacy of Louis Pasteur

One of the greatest French scientists was Louis Pasteur, who was born in the city of Dôle in 1822. Though his background was modest (his father was a leather tanner), he became Dean of Science at the University of Lille and a member of the French Academy. He often visited the distilleries in northeastern France and was fascinated by the fermentation process. He discovered that fermentation was due to a microorganism which could be controlled through methods of sterilization. Then he proved that "spontaneous life" was a false belief, and that "good" and "bad" germs existed. He developed the science of microbiology. In his anthrax studies he made fundamental contributions to agriculture and cattle raising. Many of his discoveries helped transform the world and prolong human life. Pasteurization is one everyday example.

Toward the end of his life a public subscription was started to raise money for the establishment of laboratories in which Pasteur could work and produce the various vaccines he had developed. Contributions came in from all over the world, and the Pasteur Institute opened in 1888. Pasteur and his principal colleagues, Émile Roux and Louis Martin, who carried on his work after the master's death in 1895, developed many new vaccines. Gradually, through generous donations, chemical laboratories and a hospital were added.

Today, besides the Pasteur Institute in Paris, there are branches in

At the Pasteur Institute in Paris, a visiting research worker from Iran (left) watches salmonella cells being prepared for study.

Lille, the Dordogne region, and at Lyons. In addition, branches of the Institute were set up in many of the former French territories in Africa and Asia. In all, there are more than one thousand laboratories. Approximately 30 percent of the personnel are engaged in pure research. The overall purposes of the Institute, which is private and nonprofit, are threefold: to perform fundamental research in human and animal biology; to teach bacteriology, and to produce serums. Eight scientists from Pasteur Institutes have won Nobel Prizes, the latest being Dr. Jacques Monod, who won the prize for medicine in 1965.

The Rance Tidewater Dam

The idea of using the tides to produce energy is very old. Back in the twelfth century, the first tidewater mills in France were erected in Brittany, and remnants of these structures can still be seen. As water rushed into river estuaries, it turned a wheel, thus producing energy needed for grinding grain.

In modern times, the idea of using the rise and fall of the tides to turn turbines and thus produce needed electrical energy became one

131

The Rance Tidewater Dam near Saint-Malo in Brittany is built basically on the same principle as river dams of the twelfth century. As the tide comes in or out, the water turns bulb-shaped turbines which produce about 500 million kilowatts of electricity per hour.

of the favorite projects of French engineers. Many years of study preceded construction, and finally in 1961 the Rance River estuary in Brittany was selected.

The Rance Tidewater Dam produces about 500 million kilowatts of energy per hour. This is transmitted all over the region of Brittany or is directed to areas where electricity is in short supply. The dam was a prototype. The Soviet Union constructed a smaller version on the White Sea; and there are other tidewater dams in Canada and the United States. One of the main problems of these dams is that they are extremely expensive to build and maintain. Cheaper methods of creating electrical energy, such as with nuclear power, have practically ruled out further projects. Yves Marollou, chief engineer of the Rance Tidewater Dam, pointed out that the dam would probably be the last one to be constructed, at least in France. What started as one of many electric-energy-producing projects, he indicated, had proved to be rich in secondary information. Many important facts had been discovered about how to handle water and about the construction of turbines, and scientists had carried on studies on corrosion. The most important innovation was that of the "bulb-shaped" turbine. Shaped like an onion, it has variable, horizontal fins (previous turbines had vertical fins) which, it was found, permitted water to run more evenly. When generators were needed on the Rhone River, bulb-shaped ones were used. Many have been exported to other countries. In addition, the dam enabled scientists to make important studies on fish and marine life.

Thus, even though the electricity produced by the dam has become more expensive than nuclear-produced power, secondary discoveries had important ramifications.

Other Engineering Achievements

Not far from the Rance Dam is the Pleumeur-Bodou Telecommunications Satellite Center. Highly sophisticated equipment—a huge American-made Dacron-covered antenna, and a second antenna constructed by France's Compagnie Générale d'Électricité—is surrounded by century-old squat Breton farmhouses and grazing animals. This tracking and transmitting station, which opened in 1962, is visited by more than a hundred thousand persons yearly. Every day it transmits by satellite hundreds of transatlantic telephone calls and television programs, and many of the major news events of the past years have been beamed throughout Europe: the funeral of President Kennedy in 1963, President de Gaulle's visit to Mexico in 1964, the Tokyo and Mexican Olympic Games, and so forth.

Another daring engineering project was the construction of the 7.5-mile-long Mont Blanc tunnel through the Alps, the longest automobile tunnel in the world. It took five years to build and was a joint Franco-Italian effort. When it opened in 1965, many major French cities were brought closer to Italy, particularly in wintertime, when over-the-Alps mountain passes were often blocked by snow. More than one million vehicles pass through the Mont Blanc Tunnel annually, and the number is increasing.

One of the most extraordinary of France's explorers is Jacques Yves

The heart of Paris lies in the middle of the Seine, where two small islands, Île de la Cité (foreground) and Île Saint-Louis, have kept some of the charm of the old Paris of the Middle Ages. Notre Dame Cathedral can be seen at right center.

Cousteau. With his base on the *Calypso,* he explores the oceans of the world, employing a variety of sophisticated diving equipment. Cousteau has probably spent more time underwater than any other person.

The new, the odd, the bizarre, the mysterious, the unexplained have all, at one time or another come under the scrutiny of French scientists, engineers, philosophers, and artists. The Frenchman is an individual before all else. In politics this often adds up to chaos and near-anarchy, but in the creative and speculative fields it leads to accomplishments. Through pride, confidence, egotism, the French individual gets things done. He combines that *débrouillard* tenaciousness with an analytical, logical mind. Only when team or group efforts are required does the structure tend to break down. This spirit of individualism that pervades French life emerges despite the restrictions and shortcomings of the country's politicians and diplomats. It gives France an aura of freedom and intellectual liberty.

Paris Then and Now

In 100 B.C. a tribe of Celtic fishermen settled on an island in the Seine River, which is now called the Île de la Cité, and where the Cathedral of Notre Dame was built during the twelfth and thirteenth centuries. This was the Parisii tribe, and they called their settlement Lutetia. The name Paris was first used around A.D. 300.

The Seine permitted easy navigation. It led to Rouen, which was founded during the second century, and from there to the English

Military ceremony taking place under the Arc de Triomphe.

Channel. The hills overlooking the city aided in its defense, and the surrounding plains provided rich farmland. During Roman times the city grew to more than ten thousand persons. Paris was practically destroyed by the Normans in 885–886. King Philip Augustus during his reign (1180–1223) built sewers, cobblestoned the streets (some of which are as they were then), and erected walls. In the sixteenth century, Paris, with a population of 400,000, became the largest city in France, a position it has maintained ever since.

For centuries Paris was crowded within its protective walls; then from 1853 until 1870 Baron Georges Haussmann, with the support of Louis Napoleon, set about redesigning the capital of France. He had a passion for vistas and straight lines. He laid out the *grands boulevards* —Malesherbes, Haussmann, Sébastopol, Saint-Michel, Saint-Germain. They were wide and provided the vistas he sought. But their width also made it difficult for rioters to construct barricades and gave the forces of order the chance to restrain and, if necessary, repress the volatile population of Paris. Haussmann destroyed twenty thousand houses, and forty thousand new ones sprang up behind the state-approved façades. Many of these apartments were constructed without heating facilities or running water. That didn't matter, though. Paris was designed as a star with a park at each point, a city to seduce the eye and conquer the heart. For Haussmann, the period in which he lived was important. He wanted the people who came afterward to admire his taste and never to forget what the late nineteenth century had been like. That he neglected to provide good access to the railroad stations did not matter. Alfred Cobban acidly points out, "The Place de l'Étoile looks very fine from the air: it is a pity that it is not normally seen from that angle." Paris, though, never was a practical-minded city.

Louis Napoleon gave the Bois de Boulogne to the city. Longchamp race track was constructed, and the *bois* became a favorite outing place, just as it is today. Forests like the Bois de Vincennes were partially landscaped in symmetrical patterns and provided long walking paths and carriage roads. Les Halles, the Paris market (Émile Zola called it "the stomach of Paris"), was another of the emperor's

136

Book stalls on the quais of the Seine attract the curious. Parisians say that the bargains are not what they used to be, but leafing through the old books and prints occasionally still turns up a masterpiece.

contributions. Recently, the big market, filled with produce not only from France but from all over the world—lobsters from Maine, oysters from the North Sea, beef from Rio de Janeiro—moved outside of town to Rungis, near Orly Airport. Les Halles, with its huge sheds and old buildings, is slated to be torn down to provide much-needed housing for the 1970's.

Haussmann and Napoleon didn't do it all, though. Charles Garnier built the flamboyant opera house, finished in 1875, which now has a ceiling painted by Chagall. The Eiffel Tower, at the time of its erection in 1887–1889 the highest steel structure in the world, was built to commemorate the Paris Exposition. In 1923, even though the elevators were operating, the mayor of Montmartre descended the tower's 336 steps on a bicycle! One wonders if anyone asked him why. And in

1970 an artificial skating rink made of plastic was constructed on the first level, together with models of chalets and other exhibits meant to help popularize winter sports in France.

For millions of visitors, Paris is an easy city to love. True, many of the Paris hotels don't have enough private baths; heating and elevators are limited in the more modest establishments; telephone and mail service is often deficient; the Parisian seems cold toward foreigners. Transportation can be slow, and to get anything accomplished can often take days.

Still, as soon as one overcomes these practical difficulties, Paris comes alive. The conception of the city impresses the visitor from the first moment: the Place des Vosges, constructed early in the seventeenth century, the Sainte Chapelle, where the stained-glass windows illustrate biblical scenes, and the Place de la Concorde, where King Louis XVI was guillotined in 1793 while the mob cried, *"Vive la Révolution!"* There are huge museums, like the Louvre, or more intimate ones, like the Rodin Museum. In the evenings, one can explore Montmartre and the girly shows, the Avenue de l'Opéra or the Boulevard Saint-Germain, always filled with the young *yéyé* set, and *les drugstores* located on the Champs Élysées. These "drugstores," with their highly-polished copper counters, sell everything from clothing to *Croque Hawaïen,* a grilled cheese sandwich with ham and pineapple.

In Paris are held the various *salons* (exhibitions)—automobile, *haute couture,* home furnishings—which attract millions. *Salon* visitors often travel to them on the *métro* (subway), some of the cars of which run on rubber tires, have stainless-steel doors, and swish in and out of stations like surrealistic dinosaurs.

For the 2.85 million Parisians (5.1 million if one counts the suburbs as well) Paris is not just broad avenues, luxurious boutiques, big department stores, museums, the cinema, fine monuments, and parks. Paris means work: driving a truck in narrow streets never meant for trucks; sitting at a desk in crowded offices where the aristocracy once held court; working on an assembly line while the roar of machines goes on all day long. It may mean listening to a lecture in an amphitheater of the Sorbonne, or examining cultures through a microscope at the Pasteur Institute.

When noon comes, there's an exodus. The cafés become crowded with *apéritif* drinkers; the talk is loud and vibrant; then, off to a restaurant, a quick sandwich and shopping, or home for the big noon meal. By 2:15 P.M. the cafés are practically silent, and the *garçons* begin washing up the heavy china cups and glassware, filling up the bottles again, breathing easier before the late-afternoon rush starts, before the white-collar workers or the men in blue arrive from the nearby factory once more.

Twenty-five percent of France's civil servants live in Paris, 42 percent of the country's students, 20 percent of its factory workers, 28 percent of its doctors, and 61 percent of its artists. In addition, 25 percent of the country's factories that employ more than twenty-five persons are located in the capital. These people have to be housed, have to eat, and

The Place de la Madeleine.

The Champs Élysées by night, as seen from the Place de la Concorde.

have to get to work on time. Their children have to go to school. In many of these services, Paris is deficient.

In the evening, if you ride the *ligne de Seaux,* a branch of the *métro* which stretches into the suburbs, you will see many new apartment buildings; but there are also many old two-story houses with small gardens, railroad yards, storage tanks, and factories which are gradually eating into what was once the farmland that nourished the inhabitants of the Île de France. The government has been building hundreds of new apartment houses each year, but they are far from sufficient for the increased population around France's largest city. Private promoters usually construct luxury units for a limited clientele. Years sometimes go by before needy people can obtain adequate housing. In the meantime, many of the less fortunate live in those buildings which grew up behind Baron Haussmann's façades. These people live in crowded rooms, sometimes with inadequate heating; and if they are really poor, they live in slums, some of which are no

140

more than twenty minutes from the luxury of the Champs Élysées. In these shantytowns, one encounters the blights of the industrial age: large families, alcoholism, problems of hygiene, ignorance, and so forth. Many of these people are immigrants from former French colonies, foreigners, or just poor French men and women who have become the victims rather than the beneficiaries of an industrial age. For them, life is a daily struggle for survival.

Castles for the Wealthy

"The land of France is strewn with châteaux as a meadow with flowers." This marvelous sentence, recalling the romanticism of a previous epoch, comes from a booklet published by the Ministry of Cultural Affairs about the parks and châteaux of France. There are thousands of castles where nobles and kings once lived in France. Set on riverbanks or hidden deep in the countryside, many of them are very lovely. They are important tourist attractions, and at some, concert programs and *son et lumière* performances take place. *Son et lumière* ("sound and light") effects make a nightly visit to a castle an unforgettable experience.

Some of the castles are inhabited by descendants of the old nobility, but usually the old rambling halls and rooms are too difficult and too expensive to keep in the old style. They fall into ruin and are often bought for little money by young, ambitious couples who spend their lives fixing up the old structures and making them livable. So, still today, the more than three thousand castles are a part of the French landscape and help keep alive the deeply ingrained sense of the past in the people.

Versailles

"If you want to understand France," a famous French writer is supposed to have told an Asiatic student, "go to Versailles." The palace of Versailles—one of the artistic achievements of the reign of Louis XIV, was described by Voltaire as an enormous barn full of human discomfort and misery. The great satirist may have taken that point of view because the room allotted to him during his visit was

141

The Château of Versailles is surrounded by sculptures, ponds, and beautiful promenades, and is considered to be one of the world's greatest architectural achievements.

situated over the privies. As one historian has pointed out: "The misery was not on view and the grandeur was."

Versailles has also been called "the most perfect symbol of absolute monarchy." Construction was begun in 1661, and for many years 36,000 men and 6,000 horses worked there. They bent nature to a preconceived plan. They laid out the symmetrical streets, squares, and imposing avenues, and decorated the halls, staircases, and apartments of the king, queen, and their entourage. Although the palace was not completed until 1708, Louis and the court moved in on May 7, 1682, and the government was shifted from Paris to what is now a suburb of the capital. For many people the court represented not only splendor, but was the source of patronage and wealth. For Louis, who loved walking and hunting, this was a "glorious setting" for his court.

Versailles was devastated in 1815 by occupation armies, but by then many of its treasures had been moved to the Louvre. German troops occupied the premises in 1870, and the French parliament met there from 1871 to 1878.

Versailles is an example of the height of neoclassical French art. It is a museum of painting and sculpture, of two hundred years of formal gardening, of fountains and promenades; it is dear to the French and important to those who want to understand what French life was about when the Sun King was supreme. In the Hall of Mirrors, three peace treaties between France and Austria were concluded. In addition, in 1783 the treaty between Great Britain and America was signed there, and in 1919 the treaty formally ending World War One.

During his reign, General de Gaulle had the Grand Trianon, the principal castle of Versailles, completely restored. The cost of installing running water and tiled bathrooms and replenishing the handwoven silk

Young workers at the famous Gobelins Tapestry Works in Paris. Founded in the seventeenth century, the Gobelins artisans specialized in decorating the palaces of the aristocracy.

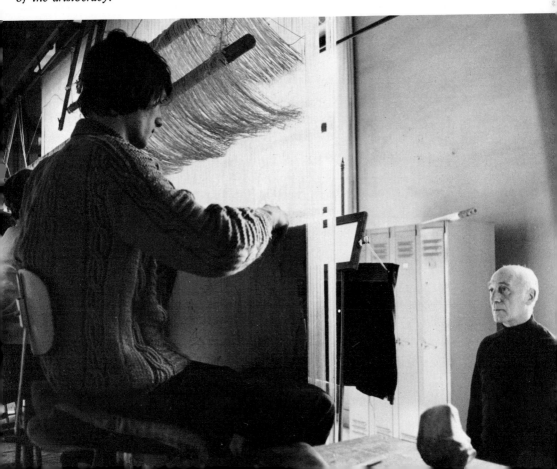

tapestries was the source of a steady stream of jokes in the French satirical newspaper *Le Canard Enchainée*, while *l'Humanité*, the Communist daily paper, interpreted the restoration as de Gaulle's most flagrant slap in the face to the French masses.

Artisans Today

In order to decorate the palaces and châteaux of France in proper style, it was necessary to establish certain artisan industries and provide permanent work for France's craftsmen. The Gobelins works, set up under Francis I, are still in existence. Today, they handweave rugs and tapestries exclusively for government offices, reception rooms, and for the newly decorated Versailles. Another part of the factory produces furniture that imitates exactly the seventeenth-, eighteenth-, and nineteenth-century styles.

For the past five years, twenty-one-year-old Dominique Delplace has worked there as a tapestry weaver. He left school early and was accepted as an apprentice at Gobelins. He was lucky and managed to obtain factory lodging. "I like my work," he said, "particularly if the design we are working on is an interesting one. I learned my *métier* (craft) here for four years. Then I passed a test and became an artist. I will advance in grade as I get older. As a government employee we have security." In the Gobelins studios the tapestry weavers are only able to work in natural light. The work is hard on the eyes and tedious. For eight hours a day, six days a week, they sit on their high tools reproducing the old or carrying out new patterns.

One of the oldest workers in the factory is Charles Daumair, who started working at Gobelins in 1926. "In general," he said, "our conditions of work have not changed very much. We cannot use machines because what we do is an art. Each pattern we work on presents new problems and interest." M. Daumair and M. Delplace both felt that workers in such exacting tasks should be better paid, even though they are civil-service employees. "If I had the choice again, knowing how other industries would develop, I would not chose this *métier*," said M. Daumair. "One cannot just live for art; a certain minimum of money is necessary. But when I started over forty years ago we all had

free lodging, there was a garden, and at that time an artist made more than the foreman in a factory."

Lyons, the Silk City

The city of Lyons is still an important silk-weaving center, but almost all of the old manufacturers have switched from hand to electric looms, and rayon thread has been added to the silk or cotton. There are, however, two or three firms that still employ seventeenth-century methods as a sideline for their larger enterprises. And a few silk weavers, or *canuts,* as they are called, now represent what was once a rich tradition of artisans. In the old days, the Lyons silk weavers turned out splendid cloth for Catherine II of Russia, Marie Antoinette, and Napoleon Bonaparte. The latter was one of the patrons of the silk trade and during his reign the palaces of Fontainbleau, La Malmaison, Compiègne, the Élysée, and the Tuileries were decorated using Lyons cloth. Napoleon is said to have ordered even his entourage to be dressed in Lyons silk and velvet.

One of the old firms still using some handlooms and the old patterns

145

France abounds in magnificent examples of modern church art. This chapel, completely designed by Matisse, attracts many visitors to Vence, a hilltown near Nice on the Riviera.

is that of Tassinari and Chatel. They employ nine weavers. Bernard Tassinari, the present owner, pointed out that since 1762, when the firm was started, his looms have produced material for French royalty and for the decoration of châteaux. "Depending on the pattern," he said, "workers are able to turn out from three inches to one yard of fabric per day." At present, the firm sells to museums, foreign governments, and the very rich. One of their clients was the White House in Washington, D.C. "With us," M. Tassinari went on, "neither time nor cost are important factors." Still, this firm is beginning to have difficulty obtaining dyes, and the day may not be far off when hand silk weaving in Lyons will be a part of the past.

French Culture

France is one of the richest countries in the world in its culture. The country's history has been marked by great achievements—from the cave paintings at Lascaux and Les Eyzies to the paintings of the impressionists, cubists, and surrealists; from the twelfth-century *Song of Roland* to the novels of Albert Camus; from old twelfth-century stone churches to modern churches decorated by Cocteau or Matisse. From the music of Jean-Baptiste Lully, who created the French opera, to Pierre Boulez, France's best-known contemporary composer.

Certain periods in France have been particularly fruitful for certain of the arts; and sometimes several of the arts yielded great works during the same period. For example, architecture—mostly churches and châteaux—was extremely rich from the twelfth to the sixteenth century. The historian Henri Pirenne wrote: "The cathedrals of France may be inferior to those of other countries in respect of size, imaginative decoration, and luxuriance or resplendent materials, but in their harmony and their majesty they are incomparable: they are the Parthenons of Gothic." The cathedrals of Notre Dame, Chartres, and Reims, and châteaux such as the Château-Gaillard of Richard the Lionhearted (built in 1197), are examples of magnificent construction.

Many French cities as we know them today were laid out in the eighteenth and nineteenth century. Town architects were forced to incorporate the old houses and three-foot-thick walls, churches from the twelfth and thirteenth centuries, and monuments erected at other times. One of the best examples of a city of this kind is Lyons.

But since the nineteenth century, very little important architecture has been created in France. Why this is, nobody really knows. One would think that the great works of the past would stimulate contemporary architects and city planners.

Since the sixteenth century, French literary production has been particularly rich. Rabelais, during the first half of the sixteenth century, was the best representative of French Renaissance literature. Later in that century, Montaigne dominated the literary scene. In the early seventeenth century, the philosopher Descartes, the moralist Pascal, and the playwright Corneille attempted to give order to literature and thinking. Beginning in 1660, the classical ideal, characterized by a tightly structured form with precision of prose, could be found in the poetry of La Fontaine and Boileau, in the comedies of Molière and the tragedies of Racine. In the eighteenth century, scientific thinking had a strong influence on French prose. Analysis was the favorite method

147

of Voltaire the philosopher, and later in the century the Swiss-born Jean Jacques Rousseau became a forerunner of the romantic movement. An individualist, he exalted nature and believed that man was born good; it was society that corrupted him. He influenced Madame de Staël, Chateaubriand, Victor Hugo, and Alfred de Musset in the following century. Reacting against the classical order, these authors believed in personal expression. Two of France's greatest nineteenth-century authors were Honoré de Balzac and Stendhal. After 1860, symbolist poets such as Baudelaire, Verlaine, Rimbaud, and Mallarmé reacted against romanticism. At the same time French literature was enriched by the realistic novels of Flaubert and the naturalism of Zola and de Maupassant.

One can go on with the list: philosophers like Bergson, Sartre; poets like Apollinaire and Valéry; novelists like Anatole France, Gide, Proust, Camus; but these are only the *best* products of the French literary scene. In addition, there have been hundreds of lesser talents who for centuries have enriched French literature and given pleasure to foreign readers as well.

Painting, Sculpture, and Music

French painting, sculpture, and music have strongly influenced world art. During the late nineteenth and early twentieth centuries, what might be considered a mini-renaissance occurred in France. Manet, Monet, Renoir, Dégas, Cézanne, and Gauguin were the painters; Rodin and Maillol, the sculptors. In the next epoch one finds Braque, Picasso, Matisse, Chagall, and a host of others working in France. These artists portrayed with great sensitivity and skill the many aspects of French life—landscapes and seascapes, portraits of the people, café scenes and street life. Their work was sometimes influenced by the music of composers such as Massenet, Saint-Saëns, Fauré, Debussy, Milhaud, and Ravel.

They all realized that great art cannot exist in a vacuum. French art has exerted a strong influence throughout the world, but the artists of other countries have also left their impact on the French. The Italian Renaissance not only affected French painting but influenced

148

France is the home of many painters, both native-born, like Henri Matisse (left), and others who have made France their permanent home, like the Russian-born Marc Chagall.

the country's architecture as well. Impressionist painters were inspired by the English landscape painters. Recent French literature has been strongly affected by political events, and by the work of Irishmen James Joyce and Samuel Beckett, the 1969 Nobel Prize playwright. A post–World War Two existentialist philosopher, Jean-Paul Sartre, was influenced by the writings of the Danish thinker Søren Kierkegaard. Thus art and artists in chauvinistic France were not limited by national boundaries.

The modern French cinema, through the work of directors like René Clair, Claude Lelouche, and others have combined the skills of France's best actors and actresses with daring cinema techniques. As a result, French films have influenced film producers and directors all over the world while giving pleasure to millions.

Great French art has been produced in times of war, peace, revolution, prosperity, poverty, and during catastrophe and invasions. Why

French art and artists have been so outstanding seems an impossible question to answer. Whatever the sources, the creative spirit of French life has endured from the founding of the country to the present time.

A French Sculptor

François Bouché is forty-five years old, a sculptor and art teacher who lives in the fishing village of Cassis, near Marseilles. After receiving his baccalaureate in classical studies in Paris, he continued studying at the Beaux Arts in Marseilles for nine years. He married and had children, and in order to live and continue his studies, he had to work—as a draftsman in an architect's office, as a teacher in private schools, and, when he was really short of money, even as a baby sitter. He never received any state help. One of his teachers was the well-known French sculptor Henri Laurens, who encouraged Bouché and became his friend.

At the age of twenty-one, M. Bouché sold a piece of sculpture to

Sculptor François Bouché is surrounded by some of his work in his studio at Cassis, near Marseilles.

the Louvre, and over the years he has sold drawings to the Museum of Modern Art in New York, and to other museums. His sculpture and drawings are in many private collections, and he exhibits his work frequently in Paris, New York, Montreal, and other cities.

Besides working as a sculptor in his Cassis studio overlooking the Mediterranean, M. Bouché teaches art for fourteen hours per week at the Beaux Arts Academy of the University of Marseilles, and occasionally works as an architect.

M. Bouché believes that the life of an artist in France is extremely difficult and is getting even more so "because no one is really interested. This is particularly true in the southern provinces, where there is a total lack of interest. In the big northern cities there is more of a market, and one can sell there; but in the south there is the sun and the people live easily." Since the time when he was an art student in Paris, things have not become any easier for young artists, and the risks are great. "There is very little state aid; art teachers are poorly paid. A few true artists manage to survive, but their number is extremely small, and many good talents fall by the wayside. There is much artistic talent that is never used in France. Nowadays, there are as many artists as during the time of Louis XIV, but they are not being exploited as they were then."

M. Bouché pointed out that the state tends to purchase works of known artists such as Braque and Zadkine; when there are competitions for decoration of public buildings, the work of young, original artists are practically never selected. François Bouché believes that art for the state should be judged through public exhibitions.

Through his art, M. Bouché said he hoped to be able to share his emotions with other people. He sold his work in order to live, but he never lowered his standards in order to make a sale.

The French Language

Modern French has been spoken since the sixteenth century. There is much slang in use, and since the eighteenth century there has been an invasion of English words, such as *grog, tunnel, square,* and *bifteck,* to mention just a few. French people who want to show off their international culture often sprinkle their conversation with English and American words. In certain circles, this is thought to be chic. However, there are some French people—linguists and politicians alike—who would like to see the French language protected from any foreign influences whatsoever. For them, the English-American language invasion, stimulated by American business methods, the American film industry, and pop music is a sacrilege.

One of these protectors of the language is the Academy Française. Every Thursday afternoon a group of distinguished men gather in a clublike atmosphere to ponder the meaning of words. This "club" has been meeting almost regularly since 1635, when Cardinal Richelieu gave the Academy his blessing. Their purpose is to codify the French language. Members of the Academy have included many of France's great thinkers. At the same time, many great men such as Pascal, Descartes, Flaubert, Stendhal, and Proust were not elected members. Membership is considered by some to be the height of an orthodox literary career, and members are called immortals. The Academy, one of the oldest institutions in France, is presently working on a dictionary, and it is estimated that this will take about fifty years to complete. By that time, because the French language changes so rapidly, many of the definitions will be obsolete. Still, the attempt to make the language clearer goes on.

Regional Speech

One Sunday morning in Brittany, I met a teen-age boy in the town of Plougastel. He was waiting at the corner of the town square for his parents and grandparents to come out of church. After he had told me that he and his father were fishermen, I asked him if at home he spoke French or Breton, the dialect of Brittany.

"In school we learn French, but at home," he replied proudly, "we speak dialect."

The old stone bridge at Pont Scorff in northern Brittany is still in use.

152

"And with your friends?"

"Dialect."

The people from Brittany are known principally for two things: Their hardiness and their regional patriotism. For many years much has been done by the government to discourage the spread of regional speech variations. In Brittany, however, traditions are hard to stamp out.

Breton is closely related to ancient *gaulois* and was brought into France by the Bretons, a group of Celts who fled from England during the Saxon invasions in the fifth and sixth centuries. Basque, the origins of which are obscure, is spoken by about eighty thousand persons in southwestern France, on the Franco-Spanish frontier.

Most of the inhabitants of Alsace-Lorraine speak French, German, and Alsatian dialect. Since 1945, when French was made compulsory in the schools, local speech variations have not been taught. The people in this often-disputed territory most frequently speak Alsatian at the dinner table and listen to German or French television. So it seems likely that, despite the Common Market or perhaps because of it, both languages and Alsatian will continue in use for some time to come.

Flamand, or Flemish—a Dutch dialect—is spoken in a small corner of northeastern France around Calais and Dunkirk. It is closely related to the language of the Salien Franks who lived there in the fourth and fifth centuries. The proximity to the Flemish-speaking part of Belgium, and migration back and forth have helped to keep this dialect in existence in France. About a hundred thousand French people speak Flemish.

Current French

Julius Caesar is said to have remarked that the Gauls had a fondness for using words that approached the artistic. This, I believe, is still the case. One of the things that has always impressed me about life in France is the ability of all classes of people to express themselves. Depending on the nature of the subject, whether it be the national lottery, horse racing, football games, or politics, conversations are often carried on with much wit, cynicism, and precision. Talking for the French, like eating, is a pleasure.

Patois and slang are firmly discouraged in the schools, and regional speech is no longer taught, even though in certain areas dialects are the spoken language. In fact, slang and patois contribute precision to the language even if to some they appear vulgar. French has always been taught as a language that, before all else, must be clear. There is strong emphasis on form and a tendency toward the abstract and the juridical. Not as musical as Italian nor as full-sounding as Spanish, French is one of the best languages for expressing ideas. This may be one reason why there have been so many philosophers and great writers who have had French as their native language. At the same time, for many bureaucrats talking often takes the place of doing.

An encyclopedia article about the French language describes it as having "an irony more subtle than humor. It answers the needs of the French mind, which drives back the shadows from reality, at the risk of impoverishing it, and is constantly testing the efficiency of its intellectual instrument." A Frenchman talking with his *copains* (friends) in the local *bistro* (café or pub), drinking his *balon de rouge* (glass of red wine) at the *zinc* (bar), may or may not be testing his intellectual instrument. But if he were to hear himself described like this, he would surely reply with a cutting remark, thus stirring up a moment of sudden excitement—which, for many Frenchmen, is the purpose of a *bistro*.

A French Author

At the age of thirty-six, Robert Quatrepoint had published five books: *The Journal of a Human Being, Jo, Oméga, The Death of a Greek,* and *Green Sun.* The son of a bricklayer, M. Quatrepoint attended school until the age of sixteen. He described the intellectual milieu of his home in Roanne, a city between Lyons and Vichy, as "less than zero." How he emerged to become one of the most promising young writers in France today is part miracle, part mystery.

Over the years, M. Quatrepoint has worked at various jobs, mostly

Robert Quatrepoint's book
The Death of a Greek *sold*
out in six months' time.

in bookstores and as a clerk. He was never robust and his work was often interrupted by sickness. When he started to write and applied for state aid, he was awarded the Fenéon Scholarship—the first of seven grants, from $200 to $2000, he received over the next fifteen years. "These aids," he said, "helped me enormously to write my books; but the cases of other writers are different from mine. I have been very much helped by the state." M. Quatrepoint indicated that for him it was practically impossible to work for eight hours a day and to write in his spare time. "A young writer in France cannot live by his *plume* alone. Established authors like Mauriac and Monther-lant, who had personal fortunes, are able to do this, but they too are disappearing."

M. Quatrepoint said that his books were read by "the two thousand readers who have existed in France since the time of Balzac." Par-ticularily since the advent of television, sales of books by young, un-known, writers are very low. "Even if I publish one book a year I cannot make a living. It took me one and a half years to write *Oméga*, and the book gave me an income of four thousand francs ($800), which helped me to live for about six months—alone. Now I am married and I have a baby." Mme. Quatrepoint is a schoolteacher, and she helps support the family. Every day, her husband writes for five to six hours, during which time he turns out an average of two pages of finished manuscript. "When I write," he said, "it is not just painful, but it is exhausting and a great joy at the same time. It is mixed, like the birth of a child."

Literary Prizes

The only hope that young novelists have to make a living from their writing is to win one of the literary prizes like the Goncourt or the Renadot. Actually, the winner of the Goncourt Prize receives a check for fifty francs, or about ten dollars; but sales of the author's books often run into the hundreds of thousands in France alone. Among the French reading public it is important to have read the works of the prizewinners. Authors receive book and translation royalties, movie rights, and their literary career is ensured. But the number of writers who can win literary prizes is limited. And often the prizes are not awarded solely on the basis of literary merit. Political and commercial questions, not to mention favoritism, often play a part in the selections. So thousands of other writers must work at other jobs. Some like Pierre Bois, a top journalist for the French daily *Le Figaro,* use their vacations to write. They hope someday to be in a position to devote all their time to their craft. Other writers are teachers or work part time.

Nationalized Culture

In early times, French artists and artisans served the state or worked in shops that produced materials for the kings, queens, and nobles of France. They were commissioned to paint portraits, decorate buildings, or produce the necessary furnishings. After the French Revolution the patronage system virtually disappeared. Cut off from their principal sources of livelihood, artists, instead of working within the structure of current life, became its staunchest critics.

Modern French governments have made some efforts to provide culture, in the most popular sense of the word, for the masses. The five most important theaters—the Paris Opéra, Opéra-Comique, Comédie-Française, Théâtre de France, and the Théâtre National Populaire —are state-supported. Besides this, the state controls the radio and television networks and provides subsidies for summer festivals in many cities. In 1947, it was decided that too much of the culture of France was centered in Paris and that the people in the provinces were too often unaware of the rich past. Several local theater companies were sponsored, the best known internationally being those from Villeurbanne, a suburb of Lyons, and the National Theater Company of Strasbourg.

Under the guidance of France's then minister of culture, André Malraux, author of *Man's Fate, Man's Hope, The Voices of Silence,* and other works, the first Maison de la Culture was constructed at Le Havre in 1961. Since then many others have been built. These Maisons de la Culture include auditoriums, exhibition halls, television clubs, book and record libraries, and conference rooms. Sometimes there are restaurants and nursery schools. Their purpose is to familiarize the provincial public with culture—both French and foreign.

Unfortunately, the budgets of these houses of culture are extremely low. Programs are not designed to reach the masses, but are often the choice of a certain elite of Paris bureaucrats. Sanche de Gramont calls this "cultural colonialism" with the provinces having taken the place of France's former colonies. State direction of culture often leads to stagnation on the part of the artist, and red tape is so discouraging that it is impossible for contemporary artists to produce their best. The tendency in these government cultural palaces is to produce the classics. However, there are exceptions to what appears to be the rule. In 1958, fifty performances of an American production of *Porgy and Bess,* given in English, were widely acclaimed throughout France.

Obviously, when the state enters into artistic production the question arises as to what to produce. It becomes a question of judgment: Should one give the public what they want, or what the directors think they should have? The dangers of government control of the arts are evident. M. Malraux, his successor, and the French govern-

"The Sword Dance," a Basque folk dance. The Basques, an ancient people whose origins are unknown, live in the Pyrenees in southwestern France, near the Spanish border.

ment were made aware of them. But in France there are no private cultural foundations of any importance that might provide a balance to the government. And one could not expect the government to provide public money for art and relinquish all say in how that money should be used. Nationalized culture is a thorny problem. There are good arguments for and against it.

The Pleasures of France

To eat a truffled turkey, two should be present. I never do otherwise. So it was again today. We were two: the turkey and me.—
ABBÉ ANDRÉ MORELLET

In France, to live well is considered a virtue, and good taste, a
necessity. What impresses the people most about some of their kings
and queens and many of the country's important people is that, despite their responsibilities, they know how to enjoy life. This striving
to live life fully is a major struggle for many people. Frenchmen derive
great pleasure from good food, drink, and entertainment, from the
raising of children and good family relations, from exciting vacations,
or from just going fishing every Sunday on the banks of the Marne—
and to be able to enjoy these things, many people actually live under
quite a strain.

A Gourmet

Henry Picot, who weighs two hundred pounds, is not exactly in the
high gastronomic class of a Brillat-Savarin or Curnonsky, but he is
one of those millions of Frenchmen who enjoy good food. "For me,"
he said, "a gastronome ideally is a person who is surrounded by his
friends and the good cooking of a mother or a wife. In short, gastronomy
means simple, well-prepared dishes appreciated with friends; and by
simple I do not mean ordinary. I mean the use of natural products

*French food and pastries are world-famous. Here, three bakers proudly display
their freshly made pies.*

Two confessed gourmets, Henri Picot and Jean-Clause Piriou, enjoy their apéritifs *with Paris restaurant owner Victor Daniel.*

coming from the sea, fields, and rivers." Every day, M. Picot eats one substantial meal, either at the home of friends or in one of the thousands of fine Paris restaurants. Although he has certain favorites, he rarely goes to the same restaurant more than once or twice a year. But the *patrons* appreciate him because he is a connoisseur of food.

M. Picot was born on a farm. He believes that this was a very lucky circumstance because his mother, who was a good cook, often had fresh produce to work with. In addition, the family traveled, and they made a point of seeking out the good *auberges, bistros,* and restaurants wherever they went.

Of all the particular traditions—costumes, music, art, language—which once distinguished the many regions of France, food is without doubt the most durable. Each French region still takes pride in its

162

special foods, and there are many dishes that are based on long traditions of good cooking using local products. In Normandy, which borders on the English Channel, one of the specialties is Sole à la Normande, which may have been one of the dishes the Vikings enjoyed when they raided the French coast. From surrounding farms come some of France's finest cheeses: Camembert, Livarot, and Pont-l'Évêque. On the other hand, in the southeastern region of Provence, the cooking is characterized by the abundant use of herbs such as thyme, basil, fennel, and others. There, the purple dwarf artichokes are so tender they can be eaten raw.

Restaurants specializing in cooking from all the regions of France can be found in Paris. M. Picot, at one time or another, has eaten the specialties of most restaurants, but he is the first to point out that there is so much variety in French cooking that it is impossible for one person to know all the existing delights. "We are obliged to eat in order to live," said M. Picot, "and from time to time eat for the pleasure of eating and appreciating what we eat. But one has to know how to eat correctly: eat small pieces and taste them well; know how to cut meat correctly; and what kind of wine to drink with what dish. I personally appreciate filet of sole and I do not like it when waiters prepare my sole for me; for part of my pleasure lies in taking out the bones myself." M. Picot believes that where and with whom one eats is almost as important as what one consumes. His ideal is to be comfortably seated in an *auberge* of good quality, in a large dining room, by the banks of the Loire River. "And," he added, with a twinkle in his eye, "when accompanied by a lovely woman, a man appreciates what he eats even more. The woman enriches the taste and, at that moment, you live for two things only: the good bottle of wine and the lovely woman. As Cassanova said: a piece of roquefort cheese and a good bottle of wine is sufficient to awaken the spirit of love in a dead man."

It is undoubtedly true that the French derive tremendous satisfaction from eating well. Annually they spend more on food and drink than any other people in the Western world. On alcoholic beverages alone they spend about $3.5 billion—which is more than they spend on rent. This does not mean that they are all gourmets like M. Picot. Their pleasure may be found in a simple *pot au feu* prepared once a month with care by their wife; or it may mean a New Year's Eve dinner in a chic restaurant, with half a dozen courses, several different wines, a host of good friends, and amusing conversation. These are occasions which are remembered for a long time. I have friends who have a sort of sixth sense involving instant recall: They can remember not only what they ate several years previously and in which restaurant, but the date of the wines. As they recall these moments, their eyes glow in renewed pleasure, and they smack their lips as if they were retasting their special repast. This is surely a characteristic particular to the French.

The Pleasures of the Past

Eating and drinking in France is certainly one of the national pleasures and traditions. Charlemagne is generally recognized as having been the first French gourmet. He ate four-course meals, and his favorite plates were spitted roast and Brie cheese. One offshoot of the Crusades between the eleventh and thirteenth centuries was the importation of rice, spices, and exotic recipes from the East. In medieval times, the people ate spiced whalemeat; Joan of Arc was said to eat five different kinds of soup at the same meal—and nothing else. Sweets became popular during the Middle Ages, particularly the sugar-covered almonds called *dragées,* which are still distributed at baptisms and weddings.

Actually, French cooking made a great leap forward when Catherine de Médicis (1519–1589) became the queen of Henry II. She brought into France many of the techniques of the Florentine cooks, and the Italian methods of cooking enriched an already well-developed art. Louis XIV, at one sitting, once ate four plates of soup, a pheasant, a plate of mutton, a dish of ham, a large salad, fruit, and jam, all swilled down with the finest champagne. He was an exception. At about the same time, the peasants were eating acorns, bark from trees, and root soup. Potatoes were introduced into France in 1785, and during the eighteenth century ram testicles were a favorite dish, as

164

The Lydia, *an old Greek vessel, was purposely beached along the Languedoc coast and turned into a restaurant and night club.*

were green peas and ice cream. Marie Antoinette is credited with having imported the *croissant* from her native Austria.

Restaurants were introduced in the eighteenth century, and by the beginning of the nineteenth there were more than five hundred in Paris alone. Today, there are more than ten thousand. After the Revolution some of the cooks who had worked at satisfying the whims of the aristocracy became restaurant owners. One of the dishes they served was turkey with corn pudding. The turkey had been imported from the West Indies—thus its French name, *dinde* (d'Inde)—and it has thrived very well on French soil. Roast turkey, which is still considered a delicacy, is the traditional Christmas specialty, along with an appetizer of oysters or other shellfish.

Talleyrand, Napoleon's Foreign Minister, sent his master chef Carême to foreign courts not only to spread the prowess of French cooking but to learn state secrets. So it was that the gastronomic spy was born. Incidentally, Carême codified French cooking in twelve huge volumes, which today are the French chef's bible.

In 1855, horsemeat made its appearance in Paris and soon became a great favorite. Today, the golden horse's head above a *boucherie chevaline* is the place where one can still buy what some people consider a delicacy. By 1870, French cooking was firmly established in its ways, and new dishes became rare. Maurice Sailland, known as Curnonsky, "Prince of Gastronomes" (1872–1961), believed that a dinner should be centered around one main dish upon which rested the reputation of the chef.

A bottle of wine is an absolute necessity for a French meal. These men are the mounted guardians that watch over the herds of bulls destined for the bullring.

Gone were the days of ten-course feasts. Since those times of de-bauchery—best depicted by Rabelais—Frenchmen have refined their tastes and manners, although few go as far as Curnonsky, who ad-vised on his deathbed in 1961: "Never eat the left leg of a partridge, for that is the leg it sits on, which makes the circulation sluggish."

Wine and Vineyards

The vine is the favorite symbol of French decorative art. You can find examples carved in stone façades, woven into the famous Gobelins tapestries, and in certain of the impressionist paintings. The wine bottle with two glasses beside it is a common sight on French tables. For the French, having a glass or two of wine is a part of everyday existence. It means wishing good health to your neighbors or friends. It means conversation—laughing, hearing the gossip of the day, talking politics, or simply satisfying an old habit. Most French people cannot eat a meal unless there are bread and a bottle of wine on the table. These two elements are the staff of life.

It is certain that vineyards have existed in France since 600 B.C. and were probably brought from Greece. Outlawed in A.D. 92 by the emperor Domitian, probably the world's first prohibitionist, vineyards disappeared from France for two hundred years. With the foundation of monasteries, however, and the growing importance of the church, vineyards once again made their appearance. Wine was necessary for the celebration of mass, but drunkenness was severely punished.

At that time, vineyards existed as far north as Normandy; but gradually northern grape culture was abandoned. Today, the frontier of the French vineyards is the Loire Valley, extending as far north-east as the Champagne and Alsace regions. Late in the seventeenth century, the Benedictine monk Pierre Pérignon invented sparkling wines, the most famous of which is champagne. And in the eighteenth century the white wine of the Charente region was turned into brandy. They called it Cognac because it came from the region close to the city of Cognac. A lively trade with Great Britain sprang up. Today, Cognac is the headquarters for the largest brandy distilleries in France;

the center of the champagne industry lies around the cities of Reims and Épernay.

During the reign of Louis XIV, millions of acres of vineyards were planted. However, in the nineteenth century, mildew and an insect called phylloxera practically wiped out the vineyards. It took many years and high government subsidies to replace them. The French, who are extremely proud of their vintage wines, point out that they are the result of a happy combination of circumstances: Soil, climate, and the quality of rock. Some French connoisseurs, who have traveled to other parts of the world, reluctantly admit that other countries also produce some good vintages. Unfortunately, there is also a great deal of bad wine produced in France. After the phylloxera epidemic the government lowered the tax on sugar. To increase production, wine-growers used the grapes a second time, added sugar, and turned out poor-quality wine. In the past fifty years, the shortage of labor and high production costs have led many winegrowers to sacrifice quality for quantity. The result is *vin ordinaire,* which is little better than vinegar.

Wine Production

If in the spring or summertime you travel through Alsace, the Bourgogne, the Côtes du Rhone, and many other areas in France where grapes are grown, you will no doubt see people working in the vineyards. Vineyards are tilled as often as eight times a year. The vines have to be dressed, topped, thinned, and sprayed with copper sulfate every time it rains hard. Sometimes this spraying is done as often as twenty times in one year. Thus, the care of the vines requires a tremendous amount of hand work, which is one of the reasons why the price of good wine has risen so high.

Around Bordeaux, up and down the Gironde River, are some of the finest vineyards of France. From here come some "Grand Cru" wines, many of which were being appreciated during Roman times. Among the better known are Château Margaux, Château Lafite, Saint Emilion, Château d'Yquem, and many others. Around the middle of September, young and old people alike are out in the fields for the

At the grape-harvest celebration in Alsace, villagers dress up in their native costumes.

vendange, or wine harvest. The sweet scent of newly pressed grapes spreads over the countryside. Whether the wine will be good or bad depends on many factors. In general, Bordeaux wines require temperate climate. The sun and rain must be present at what is referred to as the "good moments." Vineyards must have some rain, and it must not be too hot either during the day or the night. Once the grapes are picked, the winegrower becomes a wine maker. Stalks are removed, the grapes are pressed, the wine ferments and is drained from the vats and transferred to oak barrels. Before being bottled, the red wine usually stays in barrels for three years, and the white wines for four years.

The production of wine is strictly controlled by the government. If the wine does not meet certain standards, it is rejected and the government refuses to allow it to be sold with what is called an *"Appellation Contrôlée"* label. In 1944, for example, one third of the Bordeaux crop was denied government approval.

169

One of the very special professions in France is that of wine taster. This may simply be the *patron* of a fine restaurant who carefully tastes the wine before it is served to his clients, or it may be a highly trained expert working in one of the important châteaux. A wine taster rarely drinks the wine. Beforehand, he does not drink water, never smokes, and eats no sweets. He may eat a small piece of bread to clean his palate. Then, he will only half fill his glass so that the wine's perfume will not dissipate. He will hold the glass up to the light in order to judge its color, limpidity, and brilliance. Then he will smell it, suck in its fragrance, while slowly turning the glass. Finally, he will take a very small quantity in his mouth in order to appreciate the sweetness or dryness, the body or the lightness, the fruity flavor, strength, and delicacy. Then he spits it out.

Cheese

The French chef Brillat-Savarin once said: "Dessert without cheese is like a beautiful one-eyed woman." And many French people would add that cheese without wine is unthinkable.

Two thousand years ago the cheese works at Nîmes and Gevaudan were already operating, and their products were well appreciated. Today, France produces more varieties of cheese than any other nation in the world. The exact number is open to question; but it is certain that even if one does not count strictly local varieties, the total is more than two hundred. Local recipes have been preserved and serious efforts have been made to maintain their high quality while incorporating new methods of production. Thanks to modern packing and shipping methods, French cheeses are today exported all over the world.

French restaurant keepers or housewives choose with great care from the hundreds of cheeses available in stores. The cheese is tasted before it is bought, or packages are squeezed to see if the product is "well done." The quality of cheese, like that of wine, depends on the products used in its manufacture, on its age, the skill of the cheese makers, and the way it is stored. Fine cheeses have often done as much for the reputation of certain restaurants and appreciation of the family cook as the most complicated main dish. It is a common

A French woman tries to avoid the puddles while carrying loaves of bread home to the family.

saying in France that big and small business deals are consummated "between the cheese and the pear." That, apparently, is the moment during a meal when the parties are most receptive to bargaining and compromise.

Changes in Consumption

Since the 1950's there have, however, been important changes in French eating and drinking habits. The production and consumption of beer has increased. Families are using more canned, frozen, and prepared foods, and margarine in place of butter. Luckily, many would say, the TV dinner has not yet made its appearance; but it may not be far off. One important change in French eating habits is the decrease in the consumption of bread. In 1861, about 66 percent of the calorie intake of French people came from bread, and farmers ate more than two pounds per day. More than anything else, industrialization and urbanization reduced consumption; however, French people are still among the largest consumers of bread in the world.

Today, the average consumption is about a pound per person per day; more in rural districts. Some people claim that the decline in

A Brittany housewife chooses carefully when selecting fresh crabs for dinner.

bread consumption is partly due to a lowering of the quality of the bread. The grain is not as good as it used to be, the miller uses additives to produce whiter flour, and the *boulanger* no longer has the old-fashioned wood-burning ovens, which imparted a special flavor to the bread. Pushed by the necessity to produce large quantities in a short time, the baker takes shortcuts. And even though he may still use the old recipes, the spirit of the artisan has been all but lost.

Supermarkets

If the quality of certain French products has decreased, other kinds of services—for good or bad—have taken their place.

In France, a store in which there is more than four thousand square feet of sales area is classified as a supermarket. In 1951, there was but one in all the country. In 1959, there were eight, and by 1971 the number exceeded a thousand. The big chain stores like Carrefour, Mono-Prix, and Inno are similar to the American models. French families are learning that the big stores save time and money even though they may be short on personalized service.

Another indication of changes in French living habits can be seen at the annual home appliances *salon* in Paris. Sales of automatic washing machines, of refrigerators with freezer compartments, as well as dishwashing machines, are increasing. This undoubtedly is an indication that the French woman has joined the labor force, or simply that she no longer wants to spend her days in the kitchen. "The real problem of French cooking," a lover of good food told me with a touch of genuine sadness in his voice, "is to return the woman to her kitchen. We should not lose the family tradition. At the very least, the woman should remain in her kitchen in the morning in order to prepare an adequate midday meal. Progress ought to mean that everyone eats like the kings of old!" Fortunately, or unfortunately, the tendency seems to be in the other direction.

Although radical changes have taken place in the kitchen and in the people's eating habits, many Frenchmen are eating better today than ever before. If you enter a French home, no matter of what class, you will immediately be impressed by the fact that certain traditions remain. Food is selected, prepared, and served with care. Each menu has a certain logic and balance which caters to French taste and needs developed over the centuries. A family seated around a table has an aura of ceremony which has a beauty all its own. And this is the reason why French people are so xenophobic about their cuisine. I've often heard French people come out of a fine Chinese restaurant in Paris and remark, "It was really very good, but I kept looking for the breadbasket!"

The midday and evening meals are one of the essential pleasures of French life. It could be said, with some justice, that the French live to eat. Eating is a moment of comradery, of relaxation, and of enjoyment. And this is true whether dinner consists of a five-course meal in a fine restaurant or a simple dish in a *routier* (truck stop). And even though, particularly in factories, the two-hour break is being curtailed, most people stop working at noon and begin again at two. They like their midday break and they make fun of people from other countries who, they claim, are in such a hurry they are no longer capable of enjoying a good repast. If you cannot enjoy life, the French would say, what's the sense of living at all?

Dress and Fashions

Important changes are also taking place in French dress. Way back in the twelfth century, social classes were recognized by the kind of clothing they wore. In some ways, this continues. The blue overalls of the French factory worker, the white aprons of butchers, the checkered coveralls of bakers, the peaked caps of the railroad workers, the beret of the farmers, and the "cut" of the suit of lower-echelon civil-service employees still indicate a certain place in French society.

The fashion industry has always catered mostly to the woman. The first fashion magazine was published in 1796, and since that time the *haute couture* designers have had a strong influence over the length of dresses, whether to wear hats or no hats, bras or no bras. They have determined the silhouette of the woman, and the way dresses were cut. A Dior dress prepared for the wife of an aristocrat could cost thousands of dollars. It was often imitated throughout the world.

The top French *couturiers* or designers are still important, but the market has changed radically, particularly in the 1960's. The tremendous amount of handwork which gave the personal touch to a designer's line of clothing has become too expensive. Many wealthy people are no longer willing to pay the tremendous prices demanded for "exclusivity." The machine has pretty much taken the place of the little old woman sitting in the rear of a shop stitching away. The wealthy clients have switched to high-quality ready-made clothing. Finally, designing for a mass, rather than a limited, market, is very tempting for a top *couturier*.

Not so long ago the French fashion industry was still an affair of artisans catering to the very rich. Many French people, men and women alike, had their clothing made to measure; and many women spent their spare time making their own dresses, using patterns bought

174

in the local sewing shop. Quality ready-made clothing has changed the scene, although the sewing machine is still an important instrument in the French household.

About one fifth of the production of 43 million ready-made clothing articles produced in 1968 were exported. In the seventeen hundred large and small factories, about sixty thousand persons are employed turning out the mini, maxi, or midi fashions, as well as clothing for men and children. Ready-to-wear manufacturers are making money, while the *haute couture* fashion houses of old are merging with one another or disappearing.

The mini skirt originated in England and, it is said, the maxi mode was influenced by the hippie cults and Italian "Westerns," which are

175

great hits in France. So, foreign influences, rather than social class, have in recent times had an effect on the design of French clothing.

Some of the top *couturiers,* like Yves Saint-Laurent and Jean Cacharel attempt to determine taste through creative designs, new use of fabrics, and cut. Specially designed clothing lends prestige to their "lines." But their enemies are the economic forces of today's world; their ally is the French woman who, from olden times, has insisted on being different, if only in the frills.

This is true as well for young people. Sloppiness has never been popular in France, and the ready-to-wear fashions have done much to improve the wardrobe and eliminate the class distinctions that formerly existed. In the past fifty years, dress and fashions have become democratic. It is impossible, through dress, to distinguish the difference between the daughter of an industrialist and that of an electrician. In the big stores of Paris, or the more intimate boutiques such as those found on the Rue du Four, French girls select their clothing during the midday break or after work. This is also true for the smaller cities and towns of France. The French woman is a careful and neat dresser, usually with good taste, who takes pains about her appearance.

After the birth of a child, women try to regain their figures as quickly as possible. Beauty salons, magazines and newspaper articles, and radio and television programs send out the word. The French woman must be a model, not only for her husband and friends, but for the rest of the world as well. In the past, the court determined (what should and should not be worn, where the pockets (if any) should be, and if hemlines should be long or short. Frequent changes in fashion are an essential part of the French dress industry. Whatever the changes, the French woman has to uphold the standards of good taste and never commit the cardinal sin of being badly dressed.

The Beautiful Land

Important as they are, food, drink, and dress are far from being the only pleasures of France. France is a beautiful country, full of variety. Because of its relatively small size, the sea, high mountains, forests, and rolling farmland are all easily and quickly accessible by automobile or train. By superhighway or fast trunk roads you can drive from Paris to the Côte d'Azur in one day; or to the Italian, Spanish, German, or Belgian frontiers. But if you did that without stopping or without going off on some of the smaller county roads, you would be missing a great deal of the lush countryside and the intimate attraction of French towns and villages.

Many people spend their spare time visiting their own country: the cathedrals, the châteaux of the Loire Valley, the Forest of Fontainebleau, the squat stone houses of Brittany, quaint port villages like Honfleur, Étretat, or Cancale. The French are frequently discovering some small village in the Midi, along the coasts, or in the mountains, where there is a cozy hotel, a fine restaurant, pleasant promenades,

Pont Saint-Benezet once spanned the Rhone River at Avignon. This famous bridge, which was built between 1177 and 1185, has been broken for three hundred years. It is flanked by a Romanesque chapel and a fourteenth-century fort.

local color, and a relaxed atmosphere. Such villages provide a welcome change or escape from big-city life.

The French people appreciate the variety and antiquity of their country. Some derive great pleasure in just visiting the gardens and forests that abound in the big cities. Retired people in Paris, for example, spend many afternoons in the Bois de Boulogne or at Saint-Germain, walking and meditating in familiar surroundings. The children are playing out of doors, riding bicycles, sailing model boats in the ponds, or playing tennis. On Sundays and holidays, people often visit their families and friends in nearby cities and villages, or they attend sports events in the big stadiums. Though the French like a big noon meal, more and more of them are taking to eating picnics in the fields or by the banks of rivers and streams. In summertime, they vacation by the sea or in the mountains. Camping has grown in importance, and France has hundreds of campgrounds with good facilities. The home trailer has become a part of the life of modern France, and some winter-sports areas have laid out special trailer platforms for economy-minded vacationers.

Still other people find pleasure in visiting museums like the Louvre in Paris. The Louvre, which attracts millions of French people and foreign visitors each year, has fine collections of Greek, Roman, Egyptian, Oriental, and Renaissance art. Its recently renovated Grand Gallerie, built during the reigns of Henry IV and Louis XIV, contains fine examples of works by Botticelli, Bellini, da Vinci, Giorgione, and Raphael, not to mention hundreds of paintings, sculptures, and other art objects by Venetian, Dutch, and, of course, French masters. Many smaller cities and towns that played a part in the history and development of France also have important museums. All these institutions serve to impart that sense of the past which is so much a part of French life.

In the evenings, in small and large cities, there are concerts, theater performances, music halls, and the movies. The lending library and local theater and dance groups have become an important part of small-town cultural life. All in all, the pleasures of France are many, and the French make the most of them.

The Louvre Museum is housed in the world's largest palace. Among the priceless treasures in the Louvre are the "Venus de Milo" and Leonardo da Vinci's "Mona Lisa."

The Social Climate

The French Republic has something very particular about it that no one wants and everyone holds onto.—ARTHUR DE GOBINEAU

One of the things that strikes foreigners who have resided in France for some time is the tight structure of many French families. I have known Americans who have gone out with the same French girl for more than a year, but have never been invited to meet the girl's parents. A Frenchman will invite you to a café for a drink, or suggest dinner in a restaurant; but it is a rare occasion to be asked to spend an evening with him and his family at home; not to mention a weekend in his country villa, if he has one.

Americans find this attitude rather strange, even irritating. But if the French are suspicious of their neighbors, they are even more suspicious of foreigners. Some of the reasons for this attitude have to do with the traditional formality of French life. This attitude existed long before Napoleon established his civil code of laws. Before the Revolution, Frenchmen had little choice; after it, the "liberated" people, filled with fear and anxiety, settled into their habits. Family life could but reflect the conservatism that had invaded the political and economic life. When sons grew up they followed in their fathers' footsteps. Daughters were brought up with the idea that they would marry within their class. There was little or no encouragement inside the family or outside in society to break out of the pattern.

As for the families' relationships with foreigners, for centuries the

Uncomplicated life in Provence.

French had little intimate contact with them. In trade, politics, business, banking, and social life France was virtually a closed country. Only the arts and creative sciences managed to break out of the restraints of custom. The majority of the population believed that the country was and should remain self-sufficient.

Culturally speaking, France was the greatest of the great—at least, the French thought so. Their naturally suspicious nature kept outsiders at a distance. One did not show how one lived and one certainly did not need to show why. French life spoke for itself. In the *grandes familles* (several generations-old families of industrialists, bankers, and persons who possessed considerable capital) the attitude toward wealth was to keep it hidden. It was not wise to show how much one was worth. And this attitude spread to the other classes as well. There are shopkeepers in Chamonix who work twelve months a year and never take a vacation. If they do, it is almost always with an excuse: sickness, a death in the family, or a "business trip" to Paris. And if they set off on vacation, more often than not they spend their time with a relative on the Côte d'Azur or in Brittany. Such "vacations" avoid the gossip of neighbors.

Behind the wealth kept hidden from inquiring eyes rises the specter of the tax collector. The government has never been able to properly collect taxes. One reason is that for centuries the government, for the most part, has been composed of wealthy persons. Before World War Two, it was claimed that two hundred French families virtually controlled the economy. They are the power in the country, and any effort to increase their share of taxes is met with extraordinary resistance.

The French Family

Statistics show that French people seldom marry outside their own class. A schoolteacher tends to marry a postman; the artisan, a girl from a worker's family; an engineer, a laboratory assistant. Of one hundred couples interviewed in 1965, it was found that most first met at a local dance or by chance. The age at which men marry had gone down to twenty-six; for women it was twenty-three and a half.

182

The law required that ceremonies be held in the city hall, and many couples chose to be married in the church as well.

With amendments in the Code Napoléon, divorces have increased. Through a recent law it is now possible for a woman to obtain a divorce even if her husband is opposed to it. This, like the legislation dealing with birth-control pills, has given the women in France more room to maneuver. Cynics, however, claim that no basic change has taken place. "If she knew what she was about," they say, "the French wife could always obtain anything she wanted."

Religion

Roman Catholicism is the religion of most French families. There are of course pockets of Protestants, Moslems (particularly since the African colonies were abandoned), and Jews. One of the things that characterizes religion in France is the lack of adherence of the masses. Church attendance has been falling off steadily, but no adequate statistics are available to determine at what rate and by which classes. The strongest churchgoers are generally from rural areas, and churchmen are likely to say, "What we have lost in quantity we have gained in quality."

For many French people, religion plays an important role in their lives. Couples may or may not be married in church, but children are often baptized and confirmed, and major holidays are celebrated. For these people the church is a source of comfort in times of need. In France, where the people are individuals, a Communist may be a churchgoer; and there have even been some Communist worker-priests.

Changes in Traditional Attitudes

Although the family structure still remains rather close, many elements are combining to break down the walls of isolationism. Young and old Frenchmen are traveling as never before. The automobile culture has extended the horizon of the French from their own territory to that of foreign lands. The popular *Club Mediterranée,* with inexpensive voyages and vacation villages all over the world, is a prime example. True, French people tend to stay together and seek out the

French restaurants in Athens or Jerusalem; but some of the foreign way of living inevitably rubs off. How deep it goes is hard to determine. Organizations like France États-Unis and Assinter are devoted to a deeper exchange of culture. Through conferences, films, concerts, literature, publication of newspapers, and organization of charter flights to the United States, they do much to explain the American way of life to the French. At the same time, through the auspices of these organizations young Americans are encouraged to come to France and live with French families. One of the phenomena of the last ten years is that long-distance travel is no longer the sole province of the wealthy and middle classes. Credit facilities have enabled students, secretaries, and workers to take planes as well. When they return home, they may have become more broad-minded toward other countries.

French people are becoming more liberal in their outlook also through the large number of foreign students in French universities, who are often lodged in French homes, the transmission of international radio and television programs, a more impartial coverage of world affairs in French newspapers and magazines, and the influence, on the thinking of French businessmen, of foreign business enterprises. All of these things are helping to make inroads into traditional French attitudes.

Criticism of institutions—from an occasional challenge of the tradition that the French cook and eat better than any other people in the world to attacks on archaic French business methods—has considerably increased since the de Gaulle era. In September 1969, President Georges Pompidou, in an informal press conference (which in itself was a break from de Gaulle's formal, rigid style), announced that France was slipping as an economic power. His predecessor never would have been so blunt. In October of the same year, Pompidou launched his *Nouvelle Société* (New Society), which was to give more leeway to private capitalists to improve the moribund telephone system and build the nation's superhighways. Censorship of radio and television programs was slackened but not completely abandoned. Of course, certain "sacred cows" like nationalized industries, social security, and medical-care programs could not be tampered with by private enterprise. But emphasis was on the idea that the economic and political life had for too long remained stagnant, and that change had to take place if France was to play a dynamic role in the modern world.

Social Problems

In 1954, 25 million French people lived in cities. In 1968, the figure was up to 35 million, and estimates indicate that by 1975, more than 42 million people would be city dwellers. Thus, in one generation's time, France will be obliged to increase greatly the size of all of its cities. Smaller towns on the outskirts will be absorbed, and the country of villages, hamlets, and farms will be radically transformed.

The government's sixth economic plan (1970–1975) must take into

Downtown Bordeaux's main shopping street is so narrow that pedestrians are forced to mix with the cars and trucks in the roadway. Most of France's big cities were laid out in the nineteenth century and are not designed for today's traffic.

account the unavoidable growth of the French cities and all the problems—housing, supply and distribution of food, transportation, education, and law and order—that will result. Provided sufficient funds are voted and they are intelligently administered, the French may be able to avoid some of the social problems due to overpopulation of urban areas which have so blighted many European cities. The fact that industrial France has developed relatively slowly may give the country a chance to profit from the mistakes of others. France still has a low population density, and there is room in the country to expand the cities. The problem is to expand them intelligently and with strict city-planning techniques. Whether French politicians will have sufficient foresight and courage to fight traditional interests remains a big question.

Alcoholism

The average Frenchman probably remembers the former premier Pierre Mendès-France not for his political achievements, which were considerable, but for a campaign the premier waged against alcoholism. "Mendès-France," many have scoffed in disdain, ". . . he wanted us all to drink milk." Even *vin ordinaire* was more to their liking.

The facts are that more people in France die because of excessive drinking than in all the major Western industrialized countries put together. And according to a World Health Organization survey based on statistics from 1965, more people in France died of cirrhosis of the liver (caused by excessive drinking of alcohol) than in any other country. If you are good friends with a French person and he disappears for a few days, you can be almost certain he has a *crise de foie* (liver sickness), the national ailment. In France there is one café for every thirty-two persons, and there is a consumption of twenty-eight liters of alcohol per person per year, compared to twenty-four in Italy, and nine in the United States. About 30 percent of the admissions to hospitals in Paris are due to alcoholism, and doctors estimate that about 15 percent of the population of France are either alcoholics or excessive drinkers. Most of them do not drink the vintage wines, but varieties that are cheaper than most soft drinks.

Until 1970, there was no drunkenness test for automobile or truck drivers, even in the event of an accident, unless there was a fatality. Even though the winegrowers lobby in the French parliament exerted tremendous pressure on legislators, a new law was passed in 1970 that would verify alcohol levels of drivers and impose stricter penalties than in the past. It was hoped that this test would help reduce the terrible cost to the nation of alcoholism. This was estimated at between $450 million and $1.53 billion annually.

Even more important than the huge cost and large number of road accidents and deaths due to drinking is the effect of alcoholism on French family life. Men and women can live for years drinking two or more liters of wine per day; but drinking so much almost inevitably has serious repercussions on family relationships. The problem is tremendous and is often overshadowed by the more sensational disclosures of the increased use of drugs by young people or the considerable increase of crime. French people, however, do not seem to be particularly anxious to give up wine for milk, even though there is a large overproduction of the latter. Habit and tradition are probably the main reasons; and many people consider that if they have not consumed a bottle of wine during a meal, they have not eaten well.

Social Security

In 1930 a law was passed providing health insurance to some people. This was the beginning of the French social security system. The law had many defects: Not all salaried workers were covered (not to mention the huge number of nonsalaried persons), the risks were limited, and reimbursement for sickness or accident depended on whether employer and employee had paid their fees. Despite its shortcomings, social security in France was accepted in principle.

A more effective system was adopted in 1945, and there have been many additions and changes in the laws and decrees since then. The tendency has been to increase the coverage to include all workers, including foreigners. Thus, farmers, artisans, and artists are covered. Besides accidents and sickness, French social security provides maternity care (100 percent coverage), prenatal and postnatal care of

Although he likes his work as a sector in a glass factory near Cognac, Henri Michelei is looking forward to retiring to his five-room house. Social security payments will make this possible.

mother and child, old-age insurance, special stipends to parents who have large families (three or more children), and, in needy cases, contributions toward payment of house rents. Incidentally, it is probably because of the importance accorded maternity coverage and care that France has one of the lowest infant mortality rates in the world.

The huge social security organization also gives aid to hospitals, to medical and dental clinics, sanitariums, and to vacation camps, and makes contributions to medical research. Through inspection of factories, attempts are made to prevent accidents. One particular problem is the large number of old people in France. Since people tend to be sick more often as they get older, social security in France has to assume heavy expenses for the exceptionally large retired population. Money is also wasted by inefficient management, and because some doctors, hospitals, and private clinics cheat in calculating their fees, security coverage was upped to 75 percent.

Despite the frequent battles about social security which take place in the National Assembly, the newspapers, labor and businessmen's unions, and political parties, French people regard social security as one of their basic rights. Though payments come out of earnings, are high, and are rising, few would exchange their benefits for the pre-1930 insecurity. And the government's attitude has never changed: A healthy citizen is a productive one.

Fishermen trying their luck fishing in the Seine. The Île de la Cité can be seen in the background.

Sports and Leisure

If you go to almost any French town or city on a Sunday, you will probably see the following: men playing *boules* (a form of bowling played on a dirt pitch), several young people wheeling racing bicycles, teen-agers kicking soccer balls, and people of all ages standing on the banks of a lake or river fishing. If it is summertime and you are near the coast, there will undoubtedly be people on the beach in bathing suits or out on the water in small boats of all sorts. In a mountain resort like Chamonix, you see mountaineers dressed in knickers with knee socks and heavy climbing boots, tennis players, horseback riders, and even a few skiers who go up onto the glaciers to enjoy a winter sport under the summer sun.

Frenchman Roger Pingeon battles it out with Eddy Merckx of Belgium for first place in the arrival of the Tour de France at Chamonix in 1969. Pingeon won the day's race, but Merckx won the Tour.

Lovely Cannes is well sheltered by a screen of hills and owes its great popularity to the beauty of its surroundings.

The major team sports in France are soccer and rugby. The fifteen-day-long *Tour de France,* a highly commercial bicycle road race of professionals around the country, is avidly followed. The *Tour*'s heroes are Jacques Anquetil, who won this race five times; Raymond Polidor; and the superchampion from Belgium, Eddy Merckx. Besides professional soccer matches and bicycle races, there are innumerable amateur events. Every major French city has a soccer team. Clubs stage matches, and spectator attendence is ensured if there is no television coverage. Attending or watching the Sunday match on TV is a "must" for soccer fans, many of whom are former school players.

Because of an increase of leisure time, sports events have become more and more important in the daily life of many people. But participant sports—yachting, skiing, tennis, mountaineering, and leisure time activities like swimming, fishing, and hunting—are also an integral part of French life. The five-day workweek is becoming more and more common. In a relatively small country like France, full of possibilities for leisure, it is possible to spend weekends in the mountains or by the seashore. In the summertime more than half the population vacations by the sea, with the Mediterranean the most important of the resort coasts. On weekends, automobile traffic is intense, and the French road network has not expanded fast enough. Renaults, Peugeots, and Citroëns, as well as imported cars, clog the highways. To the dismay of hotel owners, trailer and camping vacations have become very popular.

Almost all of the French now have one-month paid vacation time per year, and there is talk of increasing this to five weeks. As shops and factories close, life in Paris, Lyons, Marseilles, Bordeaux, Strasbourg, and other cities during July and August is reduced to a minimum.

The round dome of Mont Blanc, western Europe's highest peak, rises above Chamonix. The French Alps offer some of the best skiing and mountain climbing in the world.

192

Skiing

Each sport has its heroes. Yachting has its Eric Tarberly, who originated from Brittany, and skiing has its Jean-Claude Killy from Val d'Isère. Although the sport of skiing was introduced to the country in 1878, it was not until the 1930's that it was practiced, and then mostly by mountaineers. The great winter-sports boom developed only in the 1960's. More than a million French people travel to winter-sports resorts every year.

All French ski resorts have increased their hotel capacity and sports facilities. Modern resorts like Courchevel, Flaine, La Plagne, Chamonix, and Val d'Isère cater to an international clientele. The ski teacher, the ski lift, and night ski clubs where the latest fads are tried out are all part of the winter vacation mystique. Many chalets and apartments have been constructed as secondary residences giving these remote areas a more regular clientele.

A private organization like the *Club Méditerranée,* which runs group trips to French resorts and to foreign Alpine areas, has done much to put an expensive sport within the means of the average Frenchman. In many cases, the Club owns and operates its own hotels. Their summertime "grass hut" villages in Tahiti, Israel, Greece, and other countries are very popular and relatively inexpensive.

Government-run organizations such as the *Union Nationale des Centres de Plein Air* (UNCPA), as well as industry-run and union-run hotels and rest homes, have contributed a great deal toward making vacations in France available to all.

Recognizing that mountain air and winter sports are beneficial for young schoolchildren, particularly those who live in cities, some French communities have purchased or leased homes in mountain areas. In the wintertime, for periods of one month, teachers and their pupils from the city live in these homes, study in the morning, and ski, ice skate, or play in the snow in the afternoons. Called *Classes de Neiges,* they are one of the more creative aspects of the French education system. Similar arrangements for spring and summer vacations also are in operation.

194

Culture and Recreation Centers

A teen-age friend in Chamonix is a member of the local *Maison des Jeunes et de la Culture* (MJC), which is a young people's culture and recreation center. The MJC organized a weekend trip to Thonon-les-Bains, which is on the French side of lovely Lake Geneva. The purpose of this trip was to learn to build and manipulate kayaks and canoes. The Chamonix youngsters went on this trip, helped to build a kayak, paddled on the lake, and had a fine weekend. It cost them less than three dollars each and that included food, lodging, instruction, and transportation. Since there are many teen-age youngsters in Chamonix who are interested in motorcycles, the local MJC organized a motorcycle weekend during which time the participants took apart motorcycles, learned how they worked, and took several short trips.

These are but two examples of the activities of an organization that has more than twelve hundred branches throughout France and is increasing in size at the astonishing rate of fifteen branches per month. The MJC's are partially supported by the government and partially by the local communities in which they are located. Their direction is left up to the members, some of whom are elected, some appointed. In 1968, the government allotted a subsidy of more than $1.3 million for their maintenance and operation; and more than twenty thousand persons worked without pay for the various centers. There are a few hundred paid "educators," as they are called, and some on half-time pay.

The purposes of these culture and recreation centers are to liven up life in the villages and cities throughout the country and, at the same time, to teach group cooperation. Activities generally reflect the needs of the communities. In some, sports activities are stressed; in others there are sculpture, painting, design, ceramic, and photographic facilities. Dance, music, and theater groups are organized by professionals who provide their services free of charge; while the national office in Paris provides lecturers, slide programs, fine foreign and French films, and documents of all kinds.

The word "youth" in its title is given a very wide interpretation. In fact, participation is open to all members of the community who pay minimal fees. In addition, some centers with living accommodations receive groups of young people from foreign countries. The MJC's are open to all, strive to be democratic, are nonpolitical, and not affiliated with any religion.

In practice, of course, the ideal is often not attained. Critics have questioned their political neutrality and the objectivity of some of the directors who are, after all, government employees. Some people claim that costs, even though kept to a minimum, are still too high for many teen-agers. And other people complain that activities are organized to a point where the individual loses all sense of initiative.

Despite these and other criticisms, the centers try hard to disseminate culture to young people and adults alike. Were it not for them, the cultural heritage of France would remain limited to certain classes, as it was during the time of the monarchies.

How to Survive in France

When I drive a car in France I tell myself that the spirit of revolution must still be alive in the heart of every Frenchman. Although they are often painfully courteous in daily life, on the road it's every man for himself. French drivers love to challenge one another—just to the point of collision. It is said that the great English auto racer Stirling Moss remarked that he felt safer driving a car 150 miles an hour on a track than driving 20 miles an hour around the Arc de Triomphe in Paris.

I like to think that French driver ferociousness is simply a safety valve. Faced day in and day out with the terrible frustrations of government administration and the mountains of red tape which have always been a part of private industry as well, the people have developed special defense mechanisms. Those who have automobiles seem to use them as weapons, or to express their tensions; they often explode on the national highways and when fighting for a parking place once they get to their destination.

The people who do not drive will take out their frustrations in talk—in the cafés or on the streets. For Frenchmen, to argue is surely one of the unheralded joys of life. They complain about everything: taxes, politics, the soccer game, their wives and mistresses, the weather, poor business conditions, the noisy neighbors, social security, and the administration of their cities. When they have vented their anger, they return to their homes and sit down to a delicious meal.

Conversation for the French is a spectacle, a part of the theater they call life. It is a pleasure and a necessity. It is when the talk stops and they must move to the action phase, when decisions have to be taken quickly and efficiently, that they get confused and start fidgeting. It's marvelous to watch and frustrating at the same time; but it's a part of the French way of life.

Since prehistoric times, France has been a crossroads for trade, travel, and invasion, and the ancestors of the French people are a blend of several nations and many different ancient tribes. Great thinkers, heroes, scientists, engineers, artists, and writers have emerged over the centuries. Today, the spectrum of the French personality includes many of the characteristics of the country's great heroes and leaders: patriots, nationalists, chauvinists, purists, believers, and visionaries. It is the variety of its people that makes France such an interesting country.

Future Directions

> In France we leave alone those who set the fires and we persecute those who ring the tocsin.—SEBASTIEN ROCH CHAMFORT

How will France react to the new influences invading the country? Is the turbulent French spirit ready to accept changes that may involve curbs on liberty? Can the French economy be effectively controlled and efficiently administered? In other words, can French society be organized in such a way that the individual can live a more fruitful existence? What is France's role in foreign affairs now that its former role of the world's cultural leader has been taken over by other lands? Is the country able and ready to sacrifice some of its painfully gained sovereignty to become part of a politically united Europe? These are some of the main questions France and the French will face in the next decade.

Today, the country is being besieged, not by enemy armies of Great Britain or Germany, but by pressures on its domestic life and institutions. The educational system, business structure and methods, farm policies and divisions of land, the traditional values found in the individual and collective arts, eating and drinking habits—the very foundations of France itself—are being questioned.

The strongest influence is coming from the United States and is most apparent in the American industries that have branches in France. The rapid and efficient way of thinking and doing things is shocking the

The President John F. Kennedy Square in the city of Brest was named after the late American President, who was well liked in France.

French because France is a country accustomed to slow change at best. Whether these methods will ultimately enrich or impoverish French life is not under consideration. The suddenness of this industrial invasion does not give the French time to ponder the moral and philosophical ramifications. That judgment is for later ages. What is of immediate concern to some people is that uncontrolled admission of foreign enterprises into France may lead to the country's economic, and perhaps political, takeover by some outside forces. It is more than likely, moreover, that the foreign infiltration of French industry—and all that means in the thinking of the French businessman—will continue. French industrialists have too much to gain to try to stop it.

Through modern communications media, American influences can also be seen in the popular and dramatic arts: music, the theater, and cinema. But in these fields—as in literature, painting, and sculpture— the French are giving as much as they are taking. The rich old French artistic heritage continues to serve as a source of inspiration not only for the French but for sensitive people the world over.

Because of the availablity of scientific journals and frequent individual and group study trips to the United States, the American influence can be seen also in French engineering methods, French medicine, and in many research projects.

In the economic sphere, some European nations are putting pressure on the thinking of the French. The most striking example of this is the European Common Market, founded in 1958. Although still only on the economic level, the Common Market has been a unifying factor in Europe.

During the past fifteen years, many changes have occurred in the French economy. The standard of living has risen. There is more leisure time, and more opportunities for ordinary people to do many of the things that formerly only the rich could afford. But greater material development and a growing population have brought other problems: the overcrowding of cities, intensification of an already acute housing problem, transportation difficulties, an increase in crime, and problems of health, education, and welfare. To handle these problems, many institutions will have to be completely overhauled. The govern-

The drydock at Brest, which, like the city, was heavily bombed during World War Two.

ment will be obliged to take rapid, often drastic, measures if it is to cope with the situation, and the people must be prepared to change and accept. But *are* they, and to what extent? Fundamental conservatism and traditionalism, combined with the turbulent French spirit, are deterring factors that cannot be ignored by the country's leaders without dire consequences.

Foreign-Policy Problems

An incidental but important result of Common Market cooperation is the apparent reduction, during the past decade, of tension between the French and their traditional enemy, the Germans. From 1958 to 1968, General de Gaulle steadfastly rejected consideration of France as a full-fledged member in any supranational European political organization, but he did work hard and successfully to bring France and Germany closer together. With the rise of politicians with fresh ideas, Franco-German relations may progress to a point where the European power balance may change.

Deep suspicion, combined with an extreme nationalism, has often led France into conflicts with its neighbors. The French are cautious people, and despite the Common Market and other projects involving international cooperation, they will probably resist any substantial infringement on France's sovereignty. At present, foreign policy is based on mutually advantageous relations with world powers. France maintains diplomatic relations with the Soviet Union, Cuba, the United States, the Arab states, Israel, and Communist China. Trade missions and exchanges of scientists and cultural groups are frequent. The French seem to be trying to establish an image of world fraternity (with France in the center), behind which hovers the old idea of the French civilizing mission.

The Changing Image

Since the French are by tradition, and perhaps by nature, very conservative people, they take a very long time to put into practice new ideas. At the same time, they are intellectuals; their language is particularly adapted to the expression of ideas, and they like to reason. Thus, ideas are rapidly assimilated. What often happens, though, is that these ideas lie dormant for decades because the French lack the practical sense to put them into practice. One example of this was the Industrial Revolution. French industry was—and to a large extent still is—a family affair. Bankers and the government opted to keep industries in the family, so to speak, and out of the modern era. They catered to the *status quo,* and, industrially speaking, France fell more than twenty years behind certain of its European neighbors. The country is still trying to catch up.

Conservatism is the cornerstone in the thinking of France's more than one million shopkeepers. Conservatism dominates the thinking of the working class, who were suspicious of the labor organizers back in the 1880's and are still suspicious today. As if to prove this, many

Businessmen and students stop to enjoy a drink, conversation, and the May sunshine at a sidewalk café in La Rochelle, a summer resort on France's Atlantic coast.

of these workers voted as often for General de Gaulle as for opposition candidates.

Another striking example of deeply rooted conservatism was the quick defeat of France in World War Two. The usual reason given for the defeat was poor preparation, resulting in lack of equipment; but as several recent studies have pointed out, by the late 1930's the French had become slaves to certain habitual ways of life. Though a few voices were raised about the danger threatening from Germany, the average Frenchman was content to work, eat, and sleep, play *boules,* smoke his cigarettes, read his newspapers, and spend his leisure hours drinking and talking in the cafés. As for the French woman, she was still bound by many of the precepts of the Code Napoléon. This prevented women from voting and on the whole kept them second-class citizens, at least as far as political affairs went. The result was that France was rapidly overwhelmed by the German armies. A four-year occupation by the traditional enemy, a great deal of privation, and hundreds of thousands lost in the war or in internment camps followed. This was the most humiliating defeat that France had ever suffered.

While the French leaders are trying to improve their world image through foreign policy, the average Frenchman is still recovering from the shock of the country's defeat in World War Two. No revolution or past war ever shook up the French sense of honor so much. Patriotism and nationalism took a terrible licking. Although these sentiments are often hidden by parades and symbolic ceremonies, many French people seem to feel that their defeat was more psychological than anything else, that there were basic faults in their attitudes and way of life.

One would think that the defeat would have given impetus to the French for the change from a conservative to a more progressive outlook. Unfortunately, what changes took place after the war were very limited.

Social Unrest

In the turmoil following World War Two, many mistakes were made; but the old cliché that hindsight is easier than foresight was seldom more true than in postwar France. Instability of government marked the period from 1945 to 1958, as all the country's political parties and special-interest groups jockeyed for power. The people looked to the past for solutions; and in 1958, with civil war on the horizon, they voted into power a general, for whom the past signified glory and grandeur and the future promised the same. De Gaulle leaned heavily on institutions like the *force de frappe,* relying on armaments to "dissuade" enemies. The futility of this policy, which drained the country of much of its wealth and deprived the land of desperately needed social and economic change, was proved by the general strikes of May 1968. When de Gaulle stepped aside, the French had an opportunity to alter many of his policies. But as the general's successor they voted into the presidency another avowed Gaullist, Georges Pompidou. The *force de frappe* was maintained. Test-bomb explosions continued on Pacific atolls, and the armaments industries kept on turning out the instruments of war.

It was clear that despite the wars and despite radical advances evident in countries like Germany, Japan, and Sweden, the majority of French people were still looking backward. They were conservative to the teeth and afraid of the new.

A period of social unrest, often violent, began in the country. Extremist groups who called for revolution or anarchy could not be satisfied; but there were more moderate elements among the opposition who were working for support and promising change. Whether these new figures on the frequently unstable French political stage will be successful remains one of the open questions of the 1970's.

Liberty, Equality, Fraternity?

Liberty, equality, and fraternity, the three ideals born in the French Revolution, have inspired democracies in many parts of the world. But how well have these ideals been realized in France? Are the French people free? Do they live in a society that treats them all equally before the law? How well have they resolved the problems that so often in the past brought civil war, revolution, and international conflict?

Much, of course, depends on what we mean by freedom. If we mean do people have the opportunity, no matter what their class status or origins of birth, to follow their educational and vocational aims, then French people are far from their goal. At the same time, during the past twenty years they have moved closer to abolishing that class structure which has marked French life for centuries; and once that class structure disappears, true equality of opportunity will take place.

President Georges Pompidou in 1970.

There have been exceptions. Louis Pasteur came from a modest family. André Bergeron, one of France's top labor leaders, rose from the ranks, and many of France's artists and writers came from lower-class backgrounds and have made important contributions to French and world culture. But it is hard to find a single French industrialist or top government official who came from a working-class or artisan family.

206

If by freedom we mean freedom in thought and spirit, freedom to express radical or reactionary ideas, whether they be anarchistic, Mao-Communistic, or fascistic, then the French people are among the freest spirits in the world. But there are limitations to this freedom as well. Post–World War Two governments have consistently prosecuted persons and banned organizations advocating radical changes in the French government and social structure.

Freedom and the Government

The government is the nation's largest employer. It controls the better part of the educational and transportation systems, radio and television networks, social security, and many basic manufacturing industries. Through the Common Market the government plays a constantly growing role in the importing and exporting fields. Through taxes, not only on personal and corporate incomes, but through indirect taxes which put the same burden on poor people as the rich, the government is omnipresent. The government has invaded the field of culture; to a certain extent it supports art and artists. In a word, the government has tremendous power.

The only checks and balances on this power lie in the people. Criticism is frequent and often harsh. The voice of the individual can still be heard through free political parties, labor unions, management groups; through books, the cinema, music, and works of art. Newspapers are able to attack the government or take issue with it, provided of course they do not go beyond certain bounds. But at the heart of things are the people. In daily discussions, formal and informal, the French can and do speak out with the passion and intellect that has marked the country since its beginning. The French are not a docile people. The country has always been turbulent and dissenting. Whereas in earlier ages this inherent unrest was channeled into war or revolution, in modern times it is pouring forth on the domestic scene. Even within an all-powerful government there are divergences. As long as one minister can publicly criticize another, as long as school administrators, professors, and students can go on strike against the government that is subsidizing them, as long as the courts can declare referenda

The Promenade des Anglais in Nice is a meeting place for both tourists and residents of Nice.

unconstitutional and the army and police forces are held in check, the door to greater freedom in France will remain open.

Into the 1970's

Torn by those changes that could not be avoided and by attacks on age-old attitudes and traditions, the French entered the 1970's somewhat uncertainly. Some people drank champagne; many others drank *gros rouge*. Some lived in fine country houses; many others in shantytowns and crowded apartments. Talk of reform, dialogue with the government, and compromise were in the air; but there was also considerable talk of further strikes and demonstrations. Common Market agreements had been signed, but their implementation in French life was painful and often politically hazardous.

The students went with their family and friends on vacation in the lush French countryside, at winter sports resorts, or along the sunny Mediterranean or Brittany coasts; but when they returned to the crowded amphitheaters in the old or new universities, the old curricula and old methods of teaching were still present. Would there be jobs for them when they finished their studies? Teachers and administrators were dissatisfied and did not know which way to turn. A divided labor movement and divided political parties were trying to find common ground between them in order to put effective pressure on the government. Prices were rising, and economists were worried about inflation. Cultural groups and sports federations were fighting for higher subsidies. What would happen if the claims that had been made so forcefully in 1968 were not satisfied? Probably more demonstrations and, in retaliation, the risk of suppression by the government of individual rights and liberties, such as occurred after the great Revolution.

A France caught between foreign influences and old traditions is full of questions and choices. Can that toddling old lady move fast enough to satisfy the growing cries of her people for a better way of life, for a great leap into modern times? Or will the country be caught up in the old web of conservatism that has so often hindered its growth in the past? France is still asking its age-old questions, the same ones that had been posed in 1789: Is the individual to be truly free, or is there to be a favoring of private-interest groups and privileged persons? The answer lies with the people. If strong leaders with progressive ideas come forward, France will unshackle the bonds of its past and once again become an impressive power in the world.

Historical Highlights

1848–1852	The Second Republic.
1852–1870	The Second Empire.
1869	Opening of the Suez Canal.
1870–1871	Franco-Prussian War; fall of the Second Empire.
1870–1940	The Third Republic.
1914–1918	World War One.
1919	Treaty of Versailles.
1940–1944	World War Two. Great Britain and France declare war on Germany; France invaded by Germany.
1944	De Gaulle enters Paris.
1946	War in Indo-China (Viet Nam).
1949	Signing of North Atlantic Treaty Organization (NATO).
1951	Coal and steel agreement between France, Germany, Italy, and Benelux countries.
1954	Fall of Dien Bien Phu in North Vietnam. Algerian revolt.
1957	Rome treaties establishing the European Common Market ratified by French National Assembly.
1959	Fifth Republic constitution accepted by referendum; General de Gaulle elected president.
1960	First French nuclear bomb exploded.
1962	Independence of Algeria proclaimed.
1968	Student revolt; general strike paralyzes the country.
1969	General de Gaulle resigns; Georges Pompidou elected president of France.
1971	Great Britain joins the Common Market.

Important Rulers of France

481–511	Clovis, king of the Franks. First of Merovingian line.
771–814	Charlemagne. Crowned Emperor of the West in 800. First of Carolingian dynasty.
987–996	Hugh Capet. First of Capetian dynasty.
1108–1137	Louis VI (the Fat).
1180–1223	Philip II (Philip Augustus).
1226–1270	Louis IX (Saint Louis).
1285–1314	Philip IV (the Fair).
1328–1350	Philip VI. First of Valois line.
1364–1380	Charles V (the Wise).
1461–1483	Louis XI.
1498–1515	Louis XII (the Father of the People).
1515–1547	Francis I (François Premier).
1589–1610	Henry IV (Henry of Navarre). First of the Bourbon dynasty.
1643–1715	Louis XIV (the Sun King).
1715–1774	Louis XV.
1774–1792	Louis XVI. Guillotined in 1793.
1804–1814	Napoleon Bonaparte. Ruled as First Consul from 1799 until crowned emperor in 1804.

SECOND REPUBLIC

1848–1852	Louis Napoleon

SECOND EMPIRE

1852–1870	Napoleon III (Louis Napoleon).

THIRD REPUBLIC

1871–1873	Adolphe Thiers
1873–1879	Patrice de MacMahon
1879–1887	Jules Grévy
1887–1894	Sadi Carnot
1894–1895	Jean Casimir-Périer
1895–1899	Félix Faure
1899–1906	Émile Loubet

1906–1913	Armand Fallières
1913–1920	Raymond Poincaré
Feb.–Sept. 1920	Paul Deschanel
1920–1924	Alexandre Millerand
1924–1931	Gaston Doumergue
1931–1932	Paul Doumer
1932–1940	Albert Lebrun

FRENCH STATE *(Vichy Regime)*

| 1940–1944 | Philippe Pétain |

PROVISIONAL GOVERNMENT

1944–1946	Charles de Gaulle
Jan.–June 1946	Félix Gouin
June–Nov. 1946	Georges Bidault
1946–1947	Léon Blum

FOURTH REPUBLIC

| 1946–1953 | Vincent Auriol |
| 1953–1958 | René Coty |

FIFTH REPUBLIC

| 1959–1969 | Charles de Gaulle |
| 1969– | Georges Pompidou |

Other Books to Enjoy

The American Challenge, by Jean-Jacques Servan-Schreiber. Translated by Ronald Steel. New York: Avon, 1969.

As France Goes, by David Schoenbrun. New York: Harper, 1957.

The Case for de Gaulle: An American Viewpoint, by John L. Hess. New York: Morrow, 1968.

De Gaulle, A Political Biography, by Alexander Werth. Baltimore: Penguin, 1967.

Eternal France: A History of France, 1789–1944, by Norah Lofts and Margery Weiner. New York: Doubleday, 1968.

France in Modern Times, by Gordon Wright. Chicago: Rand McNally, 1966.

To Lose a Battle: France 1940, by Alistair Horne. Boston: Little, Brown, 1969.

The French: How They Live and Work, by Joseph T. Carroll. New York: Praeger, 1969.

The French, Portrait of a People, by Sanche de Gramont. New York: Putnam's, 1969.

The French Revolution, by J. M. Thompson. New York: Galaxy, 1966.

The General! by Pierre Galante. New York: Random House, 1968.

A History of Europe, by Henri Pirenne. New York: Doubleday, 1965.

A History of Modern France, by Alfred Cobban. 3 vols. in 1. New York: Braziller, 1965.

1940, The Fall of France, by André Beaufré. New York: Knopf, 1968.

Strange Defeat, by Marc Bloch. New York: Octagon, 1967.

Why France Fell: The Defeat of the French Army in 1940, by Guy Chapman. New York: Holt, Rinehart & Winston, 1969.

Index

221

222

HARVEY EDWARDS, his wife, and their two young sons make their home in Chamonix, France. He feels that his twelve-year residence in France has given him insights into the French character that not many American writers have. As a free-lance writer, reporter, and photographer, he has traveled all over Europe and most of the United States. He covered the 1964 and 1968 Winter Olympic Games at Innsbrück and Grenoble, and was on special assignment for the Olympic Games at Mexico City in 1968. Mr. Edwards graduated from Bard College and did graduate work at Harvard, Columbia, and the State University of Iowa. He is also the author of another "World Neighbors" book, SCANDINAVIA: The Challenge of Welfare.

World Neighbors

Written to introduce the reader to his contemporaries in other lands and to sketch the background needed for an understanding of the world today, these books are well-documented, revealing presentations. Based on firsthand knowledge of the country and illustrated with unusual photographs, the text is informal and inviting. Geographical, historical, and cultural data are woven unobtrusively into accounts of daily life. Maps, working index, chronology, and bibliography are useful additions.

ALASKA: Pioneer State, by Norma Spring
THE ARAB MIDDLE EAST, by Larry Henderson
ARGENTINA, PARAGUAY & URUGUAY, by Axel Hornos
AUSTRALIA & NEW ZEALAND, by Lyn Harrington
AUSTRIA & SWITZERLAND: Alpine Countries, by Bernadine Bailey
BRAZIL: Awakening Giant, by Kathleen Seegers
CANADA: Young Giant of the North, by Adelaide Leitch
CENTRAL AFRICA: The New World of Tomorrow, by Glenn D. Kittler
CENTRAL AMERICA: Lands Seeking Unity, by Charles Paul May
CHILE: Progress on Trial, by Charles Paul May
CHINA & THE CHINESE, by Lyn Harrington
CZECHOSLOVAKIA, HUNGARY, POLAND, by Ivan & Mary Volgyes
EGYPT AND THE SUDAN: Countries of the Nile, by Larry Henderson
FRANCE AND THE FRENCH, by Harvey Edwards
GERMANY: A Divided Nation, by Alma & Edward Homze
GREECE & THE GREEKS, by Lyn Harrington
INDIA: Land of Rivers, by L. Winifred Bryce
IRELAND: The Edge of Europe, by Arnold Dobrin
ISRAEL: New People in an Old Land, by Lily Edelman
ITALY: Modern Renaissance, by Arnold Dobrin
JAPAN: Crossroads of East and West, by Ruth Kirk
THE LOW COUNTRIES: Gateways to Europe, by Roland Wolseley
MEDITERRANEAN AFRICA: Four Muslim Nations, by Glenn D. Kittler
MEXICO: Land of Hidden Treasure, by Ellis Credle
PERU, BOLIVIA, ECUADOR: The Indian Andes, by Charles Paul May
SCANDINAVIA: The Challenge of Welfare, by Harvey Edwards
THE SOVIET UNION: A View from Within, by Franklin Folsom
SPAIN & PORTUGAL: Iberian Portrait, by Daniel Madden
THE UNITED KINGDOM: A New Britain, by Marian Moore
VIETNAM and Countries of the Mekong, Second Edition, by Larry Henderson
THE WEST INDIES: Islands in the Sun, by Wilfred Cartey
YUGOSLAVIA, ROMANIA, BULGARIA, by Lila Perl